# How the Bible Came to Be

## Part 2

Through the Bible With

Lance Lambert

# How the Bible Came to Be

## Part 2

### Through the Bible with

### Lance Lambert

## LANCE LAMBERT MINISTRIES

Richmond, Virginia, USA

ISBN:978-1-68389-103-1
www.lancelambert.org

# Contents

Introduction ........................................................................7
1. The Text of the Bible ........................................................9
2. The Ancient Manuscripts of the Bible .............................35
3. The History of the English Bible.....................................65
4. Modern Versions of the English Bible ............................97
5. How to Study the Bible .................................................133
6. Taking the Bible Seriously .............................................165
Study Guides ....................................................................191

# Introduction

During his days at Halford House, in Richmond, Surrey, England, Lance Lambert gave a series of messages on how the Bible came into being. These messages have been a great help to many people to establish a clear understanding of the Word of God and its solid foundation for faith.

In part 1 of How the Bible Came to Be, Lance looks at the matter of its authority, inspiration, and revelation, as well as its aim, scope, structure, and growth.

In this book, part 2, he deals with the text and transmission of the Bible over the centuries and the history of the English versions of the Bible up to the early 1960s when the messages were given. The concluding two chapters are devoted to considering the way to approach personal Bible reading and the study of God's Word. In the back are some study guides that Lance put together from his notes to go alongside these teachings.

As Lance prayed: "Lord ... make us a people who really do know something of the inward meaning of Thy Word ... that we might forever appreciate the cost and the sacrifice behind it and may treat it with the reverence it deserves." Amen.

# 1.
# The Text of the Bible

We are going to look at the text of the Bible, that is, the text in Hebrew and Greek from which we get our translation in English of the Bible. Under the heading of the text of the Bible we will consider the original languages of the text, its transmission over the centuries, and the ancient manuscripts containing that text. It has been the concern of scholars over the centuries to ascertain the exact text of Scripture as it originally existed, and we call these studies *textual criticism*. This is not what is often called higher criticism. We give to this particular kind of science the name textual criticism. It is a science, not confined to the Bible alone, but applied to many kinds of literature. Its aim is to determine the original text by studying all the available manuscripts, material, and evidences, and somehow to come to a conclusion as to what was the original text. That is what we are going to look at. It is a highly technical subject, and I can only pass on to you certain things that I have culled and learned and make some observations of them.

# The Original Text of the Bible

First of all, let's look at the languages which have been used in the original text of the Bible. At one time it was confidently thought that nothing was written before the time of Moses. In fact, writing itself had not even been thought of before that time. Many even went so far as to suggest that writing did not exist in the time of Moses and for quite a time after his death. Now however, we know with certainty that men have written for at least five thousand years, for we have actual specimens of their writings of that age.

It was a very strong Jewish tradition that men began to write in the generation immediately following Adam. They did not believe that Adam actually wrote, but they did believe that in the generation immediately succeeding Adam, men began to write. In particular, the Jewish rabbis focused attention upon Enoch whom they said was the one God singled out to write down the first records of God's revelation, which we now have contained in Genesis 1–4. It was considered by the Jews in our Lord's day that Enoch was responsible for their writing. Whatever we might say, whatever we might feel about the question of writing and who wrote the first chapters of Genesis, the subject of writing is very important to us. Why? Because the Bible is God's Word written. This is very, very important for us to understand. It is not just God's Word spoken. The Bible is God's Word written. We are told explicitly that Moses wrote at least part of the first five books of the Bible. Here are some of the references:

> *"And the Lord said to Moses, Write this as a memorial in*
> *a book, and recite it in the ears of Joshua." Exodus 17:14*

*"And Moses wrote all the words of the Lord." Exodus 24:4*

*"And the Lord said unto Moses, Write thou these words...*
*When Moses came down from mount Sinai with the two*
*tables of the testimony in his hand." Exodus 34:27a, 29a*

*"And Moses wrote their goings out according to their*
*journeys by the commandment of the Lord." Numbers 33:2*

*"And Moses wrote this law, and gave it to the priests the*
*sons of Levi ... So Moses wrote this song the same day,*
*and taught it to the people of Israel ... When Moses had*
*finished writing the words of this law in a book, to the*
*very end, Moses commanded the Levites, who carried*
*the ark of the covenant of the Lord, Take this book of the*
*law, and put it by the side of the ark of the covenant of*
*the Lord your God." Deuteronomy 31:9a, 22, 24–26a*

So the Bible explicitly tells us that Moses wrote at least part, if not a great deal more than just part, of the first five books of the Bible, which we call the Pentateuch. It is more than just possible that Genesis, in particular, is based on a number of very ancient records written on clay tablets and in a language or languages other than Hebrew. It is more than just possible that Genesis, in fact, is based on a whole number of very, very ancient and primitive records written or inscribed on clay tablets. If this is the case, Moses was not only a compiler and editor but he was a translator as well. Again, this might explain why in one or two cases he does put a little gloss in and gives some further explanation of the meaning of some name or something else.

## Sources Used to Compile the Bible

We have, of course, in the Bible a number of sources used in compiling the Scriptures which have completely vanished. We will look at just a few of them.

Numbers 21:14a: "Wherefore it is said in the book of the Wars of the Lord ..." What is this book of the Wars of the Lord? We do not know. It has completely vanished, but it was evidently a source for this song that we have in Numbers 21. It has vanished.

Joshua 10:13b: "... Is this not written in the book of Jasher? And the sun stayed in the midst of heaven, and hasted not to go down about a whole day." This little poem that goes before that verse which we have in verses 12–13 is written in the book of Jasher. What is the book of Jasher? It has vanished, so we do not know, but it was a source that whoever wrote Joshua used in compiling this book.

II Samuel 1:18: "(And he bade them teach the children of Judah the song of the bow: behold, it is written in the book of Jasher)."

II Chronicles 9:29: "Now the rest of the acts of Solomon from first to last, are they not written in the history of Nathan the prophet, and in the prophecy of Ahijah the Shilonite, and in the visions of Iddo the seer concerning Jeroboam the son of Nebat?"

All of these sources have vanished. There are a number of others mentioned in Samuel, Kings, Chronicles that have been written, and some which we no longer have because they have vanished, but these are old sources that were used in compiling the scripture. They have gone from us.

## Languages of the Text of the Bible

There are three languages used in the text of the Bible—Hebrew, Aramaic, and Greek. Nearly the whole Old Testament is in Hebrew with a very small number of passages, comparatively speaking, in Aramaic, while the whole of the New Testament is in Greek without exception.

### The Hebrew Language

Let's look at these languages. The first is Hebrew, which belongs to the Semitic family of languages and its western group. There is the northern group—Amorite and Aramaic; the western group—Canaanite, Moabite, Phoenician, and Hebrew; the eastern group—the languages of Babylon, Assyria, and Arcadia, and the southern group—the languages of Arabia and Ethiopia. The most widely spoken Semitic language today is Arabic.

Hebrew belongs to the western group of the family of languages (see study guide page 192), the group which includes Canaanite, Moabite, and Phoenician. It is not called Hebrew in the Old Testament, but it is called variously the "language" or "lip of Canaan" (Isaiah 19:18), "the Jews' language" (Isaiah 36:11 and Nehemiah 13:24). But never is it referred to in the Old Testament as Hebrew. In the New Testament we do find two references to the Hebrew language, meaning Hebrew and not Aramaic, in Revelation 9:11 and 16:16 where it expressly says, "in the Hebrew tongue."

After the return from exile, Aramaic gradually became the vernacular of the people. Hebrew remained the sacred language of the nation rather like Latin in the Roman Catholic Church. No one speaks Latin except the Roman Catholic priests, but if there is a Vatican council the whole thing is conducted in Latin as a sacred language, a religious language. In this way, when the Jews returned from exile to the Promised Land, to Jerusalem, Aramaic took over gradually as the colloquial language of the people. It was the language in which all commerce and all life was conducted. However, Hebrew remained the language of religion, and it was in Hebrew that the rabbis discussed and debated, and all Jews like debate. It was in Hebrew that they wrote everything. Hebrew has never died out. Today the big Israeli daily papers are written in Hebrew and it has again become one of the modern languages of the world. It is the official language of Israel. The revival that there has been of the Hebrew language is quite amazing.

Most of the Old Testament is in Hebrew. It is a peculiarly beautiful language. It is not abstract. It is not vague. It is absolutely concrete. In some amazing way the Lord chose Hebrew rather than some of the other languages as the medium for His revelation. It would be a very interesting study for someone better qualified than I, to explain just how the ideas in God's revelation are more able to be translated from Hebrew than perhaps some other language. I can think of some languages where it would have given us a terrible headache to translate them into all the languages of the world. But in some strange way Hebrew has lent itself to translation into nearly every tongue of the world.

## The Aramaic Language

The second great language of the Bible is Aramaic. Aramaic is again a Semitic language and it belongs to the northern group of those languages including Amorite. In the Old Testament, it is called the Syriac language. In Daniel 2:4 it says that he spoke in "the Syriac tongue." It is often referred to in old books as Chaldee, quite mistakenly. However, you often see old Chaldee dictionaries, partly because of this reference in Daniel 2:4, where it speaks of the Chaldeans coming to the king and speaking in the Syriac language. In fact, it was the language of Syria and the upper regions of the Euphrates. It seems that by the eighth century BC and certainly by King Sennacherib's day in the seventh century, Aramaic was the diplomatic language of the Assyrian Empire. The evidence for that is in II Kings 18:26 where you will find the remarkable story of Rabshakeh (a wonderful name, wonderful title). He was the Assyrian who stood below the walls of Jerusalem and insisted on shouting in Hebrew to King Hezekiah and his government. The account in verse 26 says, "Then said Eliakim the son of Hilkiah, and Shebnah, and Joah, unto Rabshakeh, Speak, I pray thee, to thy servants in the Aramaic language; for we understand it: and speak not with us in the Jews' language in the ears of the people that are on the wall."

Of course, Rabshakeh did not listen to that, for his whole purpose in speaking in Hebrew was to frighten the people of Jerusalem. But the diplomatic language of the day was Aramaic, and really all that King Hezekiah's government was saying was: Rabshakeh, cup bearer of the king of Assyria, "Will you please obey the international laws and speak in the diplomatic language? Refrain from speaking in Hebrew and confine yourself to Aramaic."

It was to continue as the official language in the Persian Empire until its overthrow in 331 BC. In fact, a certain form of Aramaic was used in the civil service of the succeeding empires of Assyria, Babylon and Persia and has come to be called Imperial Aramaic. This kind of Aramaic was a kind of "Officialese" Aramaic. (Officialese has come to be part of the jargon for civil service.) Scholars have given it the name of Imperial Aramaic or Empire Aramaic or Kings' Aramaic. You can find an example of that in Ezra where certain documents given in Aramaic are given in the civil service language of the Persian Empire. They are in what we call Imperial Aramaic.

As we have said already, after the return from Babylon, Aramaic gradually superseded Hebrew as the spoken language of Palestine and remained so until the seventh century AD. This does not mean that Aramaic is a younger language than Hebrew. In fact, it would seem clear that it was the original language of the patriarchs. In other words, Abraham probably spoke Aramaic; it was his own mother tongue before he adopted Hebrew when he moved to the land. This is very interesting because of a verse in Genesis, which tells us when Laban and Jacob parted, they built a cairn (a mound) of stones; one of them called it one name and the other called it the other name. Laban, being Jacob's uncle, called it by an Aramaic name, but Jacob called it by a Hebrew name. So it would seem that Jacob's family originally spoke Aramaic. Now again this is very interesting, but we have to leave it.

What is in Aramaic in the Old Testament? One name in Genesis 31:47 is in Aramaic. One verse in Jeremiah 10:11 is in Aramaic. This is most interesting that only one verse out of the longest book in the Bible (Jeremiah) should be in Aramaic. In Daniel, chapters 2:4–7:28 a very large portion of this passage is in Aramaic. Of course, Daniel spoke Aramaic very easily because he was prime minister, more or less, of the Persian Empire and had to be thoroughly versed in Aramaic as well as Hebrew. Certain portions of Ezra are in Aramaic from chapters 4:3–6:18, and chapter 7:12–26. In the Revised Version and even in the Authorized Version you will see in the margin a little number in the text that says, "In Aramaic from here until so and so." Those are the Aramaic portions of God's Word.

Aramaic was the language spoken not only by the people of God when they returned from Babylon, but it was the language spoken everywhere by everyone in the New Testament days in Palestine. It was, in fact, the language of our Lord Jesus. He never spoke Hebrew; He spoke Aramaic. It was the language of the apostles, and it was the language of the early church in Palestine; they spoke Aramaic. We have some evidence of this in the Aramaic words that have still come to us in our New Testament.

Let's look at them. In Mark 5:41, remember when the Lord Jesus said to the little girl to arise, He said, "Talitha cumi," which is Aramaic not Hebrew.

In Mark 7:34, it is "Ephphatha, Be opened," when He spoke in Aramaic to the man whose ears were stopped.

Again in Mark 15:34, there is that great cry: "Eloi, Eloi, lama sabachthani." That is Aramaic, not Hebrew. "My God, my God, why hast thou forsaken me?"

Acts 1:19: "Akeldama," the field of blood where Judas went and hanged himself and was buried.

In 1 Corinthians 16:22, the word "Maranatha" is in fact not a Hebrew word, nor a Greek word; it is an Aramaic word: "till the Lord come" or "the Lord come."

There are some other Aramaic words in the New Testament as well. "Mammon" is an Aramaic word. "Abba" is not a Hebrew word; it is in fact an Aramaic word taken over by all Hebrews as well. "Golgotha" is an Aramaic word, and "Gabbatha," the pavement where the Lord was stripped and beaten. All these words are Aramaic.

The Greek of the Gospels and some parts of Acts suggest their Aramaic background and the possibility of older Aramaic records being used in their writing. For example, Luke 1:5–2:52 seemed to have an Aramaic document behind it, which was translated into Greek.

It may surprise some of you that even to this day Aramaic is still spoken in some parts of the world by certain Iraqi Christians, Persian Christians, and Syrian Christians.

## The Greek Language

The third language of the text of the Bible is Greek, for it was neither Aramaic nor Hebrew that was used for writing the New Testament. This is rather remarkable considering that everything began with Aramaic speakers in an Aramaic background. Yet it was Greek that was used as the medium for the New Testament. From the time that Alexander the Great conquered the Persian Empire in 331 BC and the great Greek era began, Greek became increasingly the diplomatic language of the whole empire until in the New Testament times it was the international language of the whole Mediterranean. Latin was used, of course, in the western Mediterranean a little more, although everyone was mostly bilingual both in Latin and Greek. Even in Rome itself all cultured people spoke Greek and most of the not so cultured and educated people had some knowledge of Greek. Latin was used exclusively in the Roman army and administration. The wonderful thing is that Greek became, as it were, the chosen language by which God was to complete the revelation He has given to us in what we call the Bible.

Now Greek is not a Semitic language. It belongs to the Indo-European family of languages. The Greek of the New Testament is not classical Greek, but the Greek used in everyday life in the first century after Christ. It is often called Hellenistic Greek to distinguish it from modern Greek and from classical Greek. It used to be fashionable to describe New Testament Greek as Biblical Greek because a century or so ago it was felt that it just did not fit anything. In fact, scholars said it was a special dialect all its own. They called it Jewish Greek or Biblical Greek. Recently however most scholars have swung away from that position in the light of new discoveries. They found some while ago a large number of letters of correspondence, bills, chits and much else in the Greek of the first centuries. When they began to really study it, to their amazement they found that New Testament Greek bore a most remarkable resemblance to it. In the light of these new discoveries, the relation of New Testament Greek and the common Greek spoken and written everywhere at that time, became much, much clearer.

Hellenistic Greek was a stage in the progress of classical Greek to modern Greek. Nevertheless, having said all that, we also have to state quite emphatically that the version of the Old Testament which we call the Septuagint, had a tremendous influence upon New Testament Greek. The Septuagint used Greek words and Hebrew conceptions and construction. In fact, it gave to some Greek terms a new outlook and a new meaning altogether. It gave to New Testament Greek a particular flavour all of its own. We also have to add the influence of Aramaic on the Greek of the New Testament, as most scholars feel it has influenced it. So we have these three languages—Hebrew Aramaic, and Greek.

## The Transmission of the Text of the Bible

Having looked at the languages that are used in the text of the Bible, what can we say about the transmission of the text? First of all, in II Timothy 3:16 it says: "Every scripture inspired of God is also profitable for teaching, for reproof, for correction, for instruction which is in righteousness." I want you to underline the word *scripture*.

II Peter 1:20, 21: "Knowing this first, that no prophecy of scripture is of private interpretation. For no prophecy ever came by the will of man: but men spake from God, being moved by the Holy Spirit." I want you to note the word *scripture*.

It does not speak of the "word of God," which some people could then say is the spoken word of God. It speaks of the word "scripture," and the word used is the technical word for writing, not in its spoken form but in its written form. "All scripture"—that is the Word of God in its written form, "is inspired of God." Then "prophecy of scripture"—that is most interesting because the prophecy often first came in a spoken form; rarely was it first written. Then it became written. Yet, in the New Testament we are told, "no prophecy of scripture." This is very important for us to understand for it implies not the spoken word but the written Word of God. It points out the sovereign oversight of God, which can never be overstressed, the sovereign oversight of God in the writing down and transmission of His Word. God did not just speak something and then leave it, as it were, to coincidence, to luck almost. God, when He spoke originally, not only spoke, but sovereignly watched over that spoken word being transmitted into writing, and then transmitted down through the centuries until we have it today.

I will give you two references from John out of many references in the New Testament. In John 13:18 it says, "… but that the scripture may be fulfilled." The Lord Jesus did not say that the *Word of God* might be fulfilled, but "that the *scripture* of God might be fulfilled." It is that the spoken Word of God in its written form might be fulfilled.

John 17:12: "… and not one of them perished, but the son of perdition; that the scripture might be fulfilled." Compare that with John 10:35. Listen to the word the Lord said as an aside. Now the Lord's asides are always interesting, but this is one of the most tremendous in the Bible I think. It is in brackets in my version: "(and the scripture cannot be broken)." That was an aside of the Lord Jesus. In fact, He was talking about something else, but as an aside He said, "… (and the scripture cannot be broken)." Emphatic! The scripture, not the word of God, but the scripture cannot be broken. That is the spoken word of God in its written form.

# How the Written Word of God Came to Us

All this is tremendous because we are going to talk now about the transmission of the text. How did that spoken word of God's Holy Spirit in and through men come to us? We know it was written. I am not going to deal with how it came to be written, but we are going to deal with how it came to us. Until the invention of printing in the 15th century, the only mode of transmission was copying by hand. I think most of us in the 20th century can understand this. Until the 15th century of our era, the only way that this book could come down to us was by every word of it being copied painstakingly by hand. In fact, we would have no Bible due to the perishable nature of the materials used if it had not been for the continual and painstaking copying over centuries. It is a singularly remarkable fact that our Bible has been copied by hand (at least in part) for four thousand, four hundred years. Think of it! For four thousand, four hundred years the Bible, at least in part, has been copied by hand. We would not have any of these books if it were not for those, thousands and thousands of them, who have given their lives to painstakingly copy out every word.

We know that in the ancient world, from at least two thousand BC, men received training to become expert copyists. It was, in fact, a very important function in national as well as religious life because there was no other way of compiling history. There was no way of preserving your pedigree and genealogy and the Jews were people for pedigrees and genealogy. There was no other way than to have it copied, and your copy rotted. So every now and again you had to take it out and get it recopied. This was so with all the national, royal, and religious archives and libraries. They all had to be continually copied and copied and copied in order that there might be some perpetuation of what was written. I think sometimes we forget all of this. Added to all that we must remember the tremendous regard and reverence, with which from the beginning, the sacred text was handled by scribes and copyists. This has no doubt influenced the comparative standard of accuracy.

Here is what Josephus, the old Jewish historian of the first century, said in his little work *Against Apion*:

> *And how firmly we have given credit to those books of our own nation (the Bible) is evident by what we do. For during so many ages that have already passed no one has been so bold as either to add anything to them or take anything from them or to make any change in them. But it becomes natural to all Jews immediately and from their very birth to esteem those books to contain divine doctrines and to persist in them, and if occasion be, willingly to die for them. For it is no new thing for our captives, many of them in number and frequently in time to be seen to endure racks and deaths of all kinds upon the theatres that they may not be obliged to say one word against our laws and the records that contain them.*

## Peculiarities of the Hebrew Language

It is absolutely true that the Jew had the most unbelievable and incredible reverence for the sacred text, so that he dared not meddle with it. In spite of that we have to admit in all honesty that there have been some copyists' mistakes and errors in words and in numbers partly explained by the nature of Hebrew script. For instance, in Hebrew writing there is no punctuation and there are no paragraphs. It is an Oriental language.

I well remember when I first had to study Chinese, and we were launched into our first Chinese novel. It was not a modern one; it came from something like the 12th century, and it was called *The Red Monkey*. It was the most interminable book I have ever read. It gave us all such a headache because it had no paragraphs, no punctuation, no commas, or inverted commas. You never knew really where it ended or began; you just had to feel your way through it; and so it is with most Oriental languages. This is one of the great difficulties, especially when it came to copying by hand in very hot weather, and the scribe perhaps felt a bit sleepy when writing out the sacred text.

Another peculiarity of Hebrew is that it has no vowels. It only has consonants in its written form, and this has given rise to real difficulty. Then too, the letters of its alphabet stand for numbers, and so now and again because certain letters of the Hebrew alphabet look very much alike, a scribe who was a little bit dozy put the wrong number down. If you look at Hebrew very carefully, you will notice that certain letters are very much alike. You will see little dots around the more broadly penned strokes. Those little dots are an indication of the vowel sounds, but they were never there originally; they belong to a very much later date. Originally, there were no dots at all. However, the people who spoke Hebrew knew what was said, more or less by the context. They were able to gather swiftly what was meant. This gives you some little idea of the difficulty in the transmission of the text. (See study guide page 197.)

Here is Isaiah 40:3, written more or less like the ancient script without any punctuation, with out any idea of meaning at all, just written together: *The voice of him that crieth in the wilderness prepare ye the way of the Lord make straight in the desert a highway for our God.* If you were copying that down, you would begin to understand the difficulties of the text. What does the Lord mean? Does He mean, "The voice of him that crieth in the wilderness, prepare ye the way of the Lord"? Or does the Lord mean, "The voice of him that crieth, in the wilderness prepare ye the way of the Lord"? How can we decide? Where do you place the punctuation? The Authorised Version (KJV) says it one way: "The voice of him that crieth in the wilderness, Prepare ye the way of the Lord." But you see what happened? The Revised Version feels that the other way is probably more correct: "prepare ye in the wilderness." This is the difficulty that has come through transmission of the text. Where should we place the comma? That gives you just a little idea of the difficulty.

Now, it can be seen that the result of such errors is to produce alternative or various readings. It is not to be confused with actual shades of meaning of a particular Hebrew word. Hebrew is a very rich language and some of its words have a large variety of shades of meaning. We have this in our Bibles, for example, Psalm 37:5: "Commit thy way unto the Lord." My version has a marginal note: "Roll thy way upon the Lord." The Hebrew there is the same word; it is not a variant reading, but it is just an alternative, a shade of meaning in the actual Hebrew word. You can say, "Roll thy way upon the Lord;" or you could translate it "Commit thy way unto the Lord." I do believe there is a third: "Open thy way unto the Lord." The idea is the same Hebrew word but it can be translated in different ways. But if an actual mistake or error is made, it sometimes had to be only the smallest slip of a letter, and a very serious difference was made.

I want to show you what I mean. We all know the English word *water*, *w-a-t-e-r*. If we were to put that into Hebrew it would be *w-t-r*. They never had anything for the vowel sounds. Supposing I was a dozy scribe and I came to this: "Give him water." I was half asleep and instead of putting *w-t-r,* I put *w-f-r*. Many centuries later this becomes *wafer*. "Give him a wafer; that is obviously what it means."

Now in a sense, this little mistake is not serious in one way. It does not change any great doctrine, as it were, but you can see what has happened, can't you? Later on, of course, the Masoretes, the rabbis of our era, began to put in little tiny vowel points. In that way, they got the idea over as to what it really meant. That is why you can see all the little dots in the Masoretic text, which indicate the vowel sounds.

This is not as funny as it might seem to you. Take the title of the Lord most used in the Bible, *Jehovah*. In Hebrew, Jehovah was YHWH, and we do not even know now how this was pronounced originally. We believe that the vowel sound was Yahweh. That is the nearest we have gotten to it and is the most generally accepted sound for the name Jehovah. However, it was because of the Hebrew script that we have had this difficulty.

Someone may say, "Now that is all very interesting, but how does it really affect us in the reading of the Bible?" I am going to give you an actual concrete example of it. Hebrews 11:21: "By faith Jacob, when he was dying, blessed each of the sons of Joseph; and worshipped, leaning upon the top of his staff."

Let's look at the account in Genesis 47:31 Authorised Version (KJV) : "And he said, Swear unto me. And he sware unto him. And Israel bowed himself upon the bed's head." How on earth is the bed's head a staff in the New Testament? In the Genesis record it says, "Jacob bowed himself upon the bed's head." He worshipped, leaning on the bed's head. Hebrews tells us that he worshipped leaning on his staff. It is quite simple. The Hebrew for bed and for staff is the same. The consonants are m-t-h, but with this difference: bed was pronounced "mittah" and staff was pronounced "matteh." There was no written vowel sound. When Septuagint translators came to this, they evidently used a text for their translation which suggested that it was "a staff" and not "a bed," so they wrote in Greek, "And he bowed himself on the top of his staff." This is how very small errors have come into the actual text of the Bible.

As you can see from what I have said here, the result of such errors is to produce alternative or variant readings, not to be confused with actual shades of meaning within one Hebrew word. I will give you a few examples. Psalm 100:3 (Authorised Version KJV): "Know ye that the Lord, he is God: it is he that hath made us, and not we ourselves: we are his people, and the sheep of his pasture." My version says, "Know ye that the Lord, he is God: It is he that hath made us, and we are his; we are his people, and the sheep of his pasture." The Authorised Version (KJV) says, "… and not we ourselves." My version says the exact opposite. It says, "… and we are his," and it all depends on one small vowel sound. Evidently, some scribe was not quite clear on this, and we really, truthfully do not know which one it was. Actually both are lovely, aren't they? This is the wonder of variant readings because so often the Lord seems to use the variant readings. For instance, what does it matter if it says, "It is he that has made us and not we ourselves"? Thank the Lord, it was not ourselves, but He has made us. But if it reads, "It is he that has made us and we are his," praise the Lord for that. It does not really matter.

Isaiah 9:3 is a little more difficult. "Thou hast multiplied the nation, and not increased the joy: they joy before thee according to the joy in harvest, and as men rejoice when they divide the spoil" (Authorised Version KJV). My version says much more sensibly: "Thou hast multiplied the nation, thou hast increased their joy ..." In this instance, it is quite clear that the scribe was asleep when he put this little point here. It seems quite clear that it has to be corrected, and in our latest version these little points have actually been corrected where it is necessary. Again, it was just one single letter that was overlooked, and it has changed the thing.

You may have heard the story about the man who was an atheist and had a big plaque put up in his living room: "God is nowhere." Then he asked his little girl when she came in, "Read that to me." She read: "God is now here." Sometimes it is a question of how we look at it. This throws a lot of light on what some of the scribes, I am afraid, did with some of the scriptures. Well, these examples show where a correction must be made.

We have another variant which is very interesting; this is a Greek one. Revelation 1:5: "And from Jesus Christ, who is the faithful witness, and the first begotten of the dead, and the prince of the kings of the earth. Unto him that loved us, and washed us from our sins in his own blood" (Authorised Version KJV). "… washed us from our sins." My version says, "Unto him that loveth us, and loosed us from our sins" (ASV). The difference here is the one letter "O." One single letter has made all the difference between loose and wash, but in fact both words are blessed of God. It is true we have been washed from our sins in His blood, and what's more we have been loosed from our sins in His blood. I think perhaps the word "loosed" has a stronger feeling about it because we are actually delivered from them; they are loosed from us, taken right off us. But the idea is inherent in washing. What do you do with dirt? You remove it from yourself when you wash, and that is the idea of loosing. In this most wonderful way you have a variant due to a small error. We do not really know what was the actual original—it could be "washed;" it could be "loosed." I think most authorities lean toward loosing, but here again is another example of a small error in transmission.

## The Effect of Any Errors in the Text

I think we can say this: considering the period of time covered, and the complexity of some of the records transmitted, copied, and the amount of the material involved, it is a real wonder that the mistakes are so few and so unimportant. Not one, and I cannot stress this enough, not one single doctrine in the whole Bible is affected by any one of these errors, nor is any one of the major themes of the Bible impaired. But I want to go further and say this: not even one of the minor themes of the Bible is impaired by any one of these errors. This I think is the most remarkable evidence of the oversight of God.

I want to quote from F.F. Bruce, who quotes one of the editors of the American Revised Standard Version, as saying this: "It will be obvious to the careful reader that still in 1946" (when this was brought out,) "as in 1881" (that is the English revision,) "and 1901" (that is the American Standard Version,) "no doctrine of the Christian faith has been affected by the revision, for the simple reason that out of thousands of variant readings in the manuscript, none has turned up thus far that requires a revision of Christian doctrine." That is absolutely remarkable. It staggers one, in fact, when one remembers that even since the invention of printing, mistakes get into publication.

I have often told you the story about one of the first editions of *Sacred Songs and Solos*. When it was just about to go out, they discovered, to their horror, a most dreadful mistake in one of our best known hymns and had to withdraw the whole edition: "Guide Me, O Thou Great Jehovah, Pilgrim Through This Barren Land." In the third verse one of the lines says, "Land me safe on Canaan's side," but one slip had turned an "e" into "y", so that it had: "Land my safe on Canaan's side." And the whole edition had to be withdrawn because it was so against Christian doctrine. Here were the dear saints singing about their safes being landed safe on Canaan's side, so that had to be withdrawn entirely and replaced.

In fact, it is not only in hymnals that some awful mistakes have got in, but in actual fact in our printed versions of the Bible. One, for instance, which I must say is a highly amusing mistake, was in Psalm 119:161. It was one of the old editions of the Bible: "Princes have persecuted me without a cause." That is the way it should have been printed, but whether this was some printer's apprentice with a grudge against his master, I do not know, but he substituted the word "prince" with "printer." Into the version of the Bible came, "Printers have persecuted me without cause," and the whole edition had to be withdrawn. That was many, many years ago.

Perhaps the greatest example of a mistake in the Bible, since the invention of printing, was in what came to be called the Wycliffe Bible because of the omission in the seventh commandment of the Ten Commandments in Exodus 20:14: "Thou shalt not commit adultery." The omission was the word "not." So it came out, "Thou shalt commit adultery," and it was popularly called the "wicked" Bible and had to be withdrawn.

Why am I telling you these things? I am not just saying these things to make you laugh. Actually, when we come to the versions of the Bible there will be much more to make you laugh. I am telling you these things because it seems to me no mean feat that with all the copying by hand over centuries and centuries and centuries so few mistakes, in fact, have come through.

## The Sovereign Oversight of the Holy Spirit

In conclusion, it is singularly remarkable, considering all the evidence we have, that we hold today a text of both the Old Testament and the New Testament, which are both substantially and essentially what was originally written and to whose accuracy all the latest discoveries testify. It cannot be explained in any other way than by the sovereign oversight of the Holy Spirit of God, who having spoken the Word, watched over its being written and has ever since watched over its transmission. Not only its transmission by hand and through printing presses, but I would like to say, as we shall look at in a further study, has looked over its translations into the various tongues of the world. I think we can say that we have enough to try our faith and enough to bring us to our knees in wonder.

Don't ask me why the Lord has not kept out all the little mistakes. Why didn't He? The easiest thing in the world for the Lord would have been not to allow any scribe to forget to dot an *i* or cross a *t*. But the Lord did not do it, and we cannot explain why He did not do it. But the Lord did watch over every single thing that was important, and we have it. It is the most remarkable thing that we have a Bible in its entirety, and not only in its entirety but in the form essentially in which it was first written, and yet the Lord allowed these little things to come in. Why? I say we have enough evidence to baffle us, to give perhaps, sometimes cause for doubt, to try our faith and we have certainly enough evidence to bring us to our knees in worship and wonder, that God has brought this Book to us.

I would like to say again, God is not clinical. I think some Christians in their whole approach try to be clinical and thereby get themselves into an awful mess. It seems the more I study these things, the more I see them, my observation in closing would be this: you cannot really be clinical; God is not clinical. It is absolutely inspired, absolutely reliable and dependable, absolutely trustworthy. Yet we have got some evidences of human frailty, and human weakness, or humanity, even in the actual text of the Bible, but in such a way that in the end it glorifies God. And that is the last thing we can say about the text of the Bible. The very errors glorify God. It is a reminder to me that the whole thing, if left, could have sunk into an abyss of complete distortion, perversion, and utter obliteration in parts, and yet God did not allow it. Not only did He not allow it, but sometimes the very variant readings are in themselves a blessing. I cannot explain that; I have to leave it. But I must say, that is one of the causes that strengthens my faith rather than weakens it.

*Dear Lord Jesus, we do thank Thee for Thy Word, which Thou hast brought to us in such a remarkable way. We are so often Lord, found to be people ignorant of the way it has come to us and some of the problems that are involved in it. But Lord, we want to worship Thee that in our hands we have an entire Bible, we have a revelation that begins and ends in which Thou hast in a most wonderful and in an unfolding way revealed Thyself. All we can say, Lord, is that we need Thy Holy Spirit to lead us into an ever greater appreciation and experience of what Thou hast revealed. So help us, Lord, and use this study to really strengthen our faith and not weaken it and to give us strong foundations upon which we can stand. We ask it in the name of our Lord Jesus Christ. Amen.*

# 2.
# The Ancient Manuscripts of the Bible

We come now to this matter of the ancient manuscripts which contain the text of the Bible. We have been considering the text of the Bible and this whole subject of what is called technically, "textual criticism." We have already spoken about the languages in the Bible. There are three—Hebrew, Aramaic, and Greek. We have also mentioned the transmission of the text, and the way that over the years the text has been copied by hand until finally we have the text from which we derive our English versions today.

## Ancient Manuscripts of the Old Testament

First, we will look at the ancient manuscripts of the Old Testament, those manuscripts that contain the original text. The problem of establishing the correct Hebrew text of the Old Testament is not at all an easy problem for only comparatively late manuscripts survive. We have no full manuscripts earlier than the ninth century after Christ. (Many people do not realise that.)

The earliest manuscript of the Old Testament began to be written at least some four or five thousand years ago, but the earliest extant manuscripts we have of the Old Testament are from the ninth century after Christ. We have, of course, some books and some fragments which are much earlier, especially since the discovery of what we call the Dead Sea Scrolls. There is a manuscript of the Pentateuch, the first five books of the Bible, in the British Museum, which is usually dated approximately in the ninth century AD. We have another manuscript of the prophets, former and latter, in Leningrad. (By the way, quite a number of the manuscripts are in Russia.) One of the most important concerning the prophets, both former and latter, is in Leningrad and is actually dated 916 AD. There is also one of the whole Old Testament in Leningrad dated from the early part of the 11th century. There is one manuscript of the whole Old Testament at the University of Oxford, which is older than the one in Leningrad, and we have another one of the whole Old Testament in Aleppo in Syria, which is even older. All these belong to the same family of texts, tracing their lineage back to the same basic text. That there were other basic texts for the Old Testament is evident from other versions we have—the Septuagint, that is the old Greek Version of the Old Testament, the Syriac Version, and one or two others.

First, there is the original text, although we have not got the actual original text, that is, what was written originally, for either the Old Testament or the New Testament. The original text is, as it were, the father of all. Then, we have three basic texts. We have the one that finally came to be called the Septuagint, or sometimes written with the Roman numerals LXX. Another one became the basic text for what we call the Syriac Version or the

Peshitta. Then we have another basic text, which has come down to what we call today the Masoretic Text (this could be noted in your Bible as MT), upon which our Old Testament as we now have it in English, is based. The Swedish, Danish, German and other languages have all come from the Masoretic Text.

So we have one original text, and gradually, somehow it got divided into three basic texts, which though substantially the same, vary in detail. From those basic texts, there is quite a lot of variation. Before we had the version called the Septuagint, which we now know as the official version, there were a number of Septuagint versions which somewhat varied one from the other. It was the same with the Syriac Version and it is possible even with the Masoretic Text there was a certain amount of variation. If you keep that in mind you will understand what I am talking about when I speak about basic texts and the original text and about families. A family traces its lineage back to one basic text, which in turn traces its origin back to the original text.

## The Masoretic Text

All extant Hebrew manuscripts of the Old Testament contain what is called the Masoretic Text. The word *Masoretic* comes from the Hebrew word *masorah*, which means "tradition." The Masoretes were a people who edited the text that has come to be called the Masoretic Text. Masoretes literally means transmitters. They were the transmitters of the traditional text. All the manuscripts we talked about—the one in the British Museum, the two in Leningrad, the one at Oxford, the other at Aleppo, and many others—all extant Hebrew texts contain the Masoretic Text.

The Masoretes were most remarkable men. They were Jewish rabbis and scholars who edited the Old Testament from the sixth to the ninth century AD. They were responsible for introducing vowel signs and punctuation into the Hebrew. Originally, it did not have all the dots under it, nor did it have any punctuation. The Masoretes were responsible for all the little dots that have been put into the Hebrew script in order to show people how to pronounce the words. When Hebrew became a dead language, people were in danger of forgetting how to pronounce these words, so they introduced the vowel signs and punctuation into the text.

The Masoretes were responsible for fixing the text to exactness and observed the strictest rules for copying. Their work was unbelievably, incredibly, painstaking. They had to do it all by hand, and when they were copying a book, the rabbi or scribe had to count every single letter. First, they counted the whole number of letters in the original and made sure it was correct. Then they had to find the central letter of the book and make a note of it. Then, when he had made his copy, he had to count his whole copy, every single letter that he had used. (You can imagine the book of Isaiah must have been a job.) Then he had to go through it again and find the central letter. If in fact, the number of letters in the central letter did not tally—the copy with the original—then the copy was destroyed. That was months of painstaking work destroyed. They did the same with words. Every word was counted for a book and the central word was discovered. These were the strict rules they had for checking for accuracy, checking against mistakes. It is even said that when they actually had the whole copy of the Old Testament they counted all the letters of all the books of the Old Testament. They were incredibly painstaking.

Their guiding principle was to hand on the text as they had received it. That is why they were called Traditionalists, transmitters of the traditional text. It is because of their tremendous reverence for the text of the Old Testament that had come to them and the high standard of accuracy that came to be associated with them, that we have no really early Hebrew manuscripts. The rabbis disposed of the old worn copies of the Old Testament by reverently burying them in consecrated ground. They had such a high standard of accuracy and so revered the text that rather than allow it to fall into bad hands or just to rot, they actually buried it in consecrated ground. Often before it was reverently interred in consecrated ground, it was stored away in a room in the synagogue called the Genizah, which means simply "the hiding place." These Genizahs, where these old books were stored away when no longer in use, have in fact, especially in some parts, yielded some wonderful signs. For instance, there is what we often call the Cairo Genizah. In one of the old synagogues in old Cairo in one of these Genizahs, in one of those old rooms, they discovered a whole number of manuscripts which had been forgotten, praise the Lord, and had not been interred. This gave us some of our earliest portions of the Old Testament until the discovery of the Dead Sea Scrolls.

The Masoretic Text itself was based on the work of the Talmudists. The Talmud of course is revered amongst Jews to this day. I once wanted to get a copy here for the library, but there are twelve portfolio volumes that make up the Talmud and the cost was in the region of sixty or seventy pounds, so it was out of the question. But the Talmud is the oldest Jewish commentary, if you can call it a commentary, on the Old Testament. It contains the most ancient observations, stories, expansions, explanations, and interpretations of the Old Testament in existence. The Masoretic Text traces its ancestry to the Talmudists of the second century AD and onward to the sixth century who by collating and compiling what we now call the Talmud, safeguarded the text of the Old Testament. It was this text that the Masoretes edited and fixed to absolute exactness. Thus, if you have followed me, we can trace the text back through the centuries to within one century or less of our Lord Himself. Indeed, we can say with a real degree of certainty that in all probability we have in the Masoretic Text the actual text with which our Lord Jesus Himself was acquainted.

## Five Means of Checking the Masoretic Text

However, we must ask ourselves a question. Have we any other means of checking this Masoretic Text? How do we know that it is authentic? How do we know that this is the text that represents the original? For instance, why could it not be that the Septuagint is more representative of the original? We have three basic texts. How do we know that the Masoretic Text really represents the original? How can we check it?

## The Samaritan Pentateuch

In the most wonderful way we have five principle means of checking the Masoretic Text. The first we call the Samaritan Pentateuch. This was a version in Hebrew of Genesis, Exodus, Leviticus, Numbers, and Deuteronomy. It is unquestionably derived from the most ancient text, different to the Masoretic Text, which must date from at least the fifth century before Christ. The earliest manuscripts extant date from the tenth century and the 13th century after Christ. Nevertheless, they embody a text which is much, much earlier. It deviates from the Masoretic Text quite a lot, but in substance it testifies to the essential accuracy of the Masoretic Text and because of its antiquity it is an invaluable check on the Pentateuch.

## The Dead Sea Scrolls

The second means of checking on the Masoretic Text is the very exciting discovery of the Dead Sea Scrolls in 1947 and 1948 at a place in Palestine called Qumran. A large number of Biblical and Rabbinic or Jewish manuscripts were discovered there and this discovery has greatly influenced the whole study of the text of the Old Testament. These manuscripts are earlier than the Masoretic Text by between nine hundred and one thousand years. It is remarkable that the Lord has allowed these things to remain undiscovered until our lifetime. He allowed all the storm over the authenticity of the text and the controversy over the genuineness of the Old Testament to blow out before one of the greatest major discoveries concerning the text had been made.

What did these manuscripts consist of? They consisted of an awful lot of literature, but for now we will confine ourselves to just a few points. Firstly, they include a copy of Isaiah in completeness, a full copy of Isaiah dated by most scholars, nearly all of them to at least 150 BC. Now that is tremendous! It simply means that what we were sometimes told in earlier days that all those prophecies had been interpolated by wicked Christian scribes, has in fact, been proved false. We now have an actual manuscript copy of Isaiah as we know it at least a century before the Lord Jesus was born. We also have fragments of every other Old Testament book except Esther. Dear old Esther is the only who one is left out entirely. There is no mention of her at all. Some of the books of the Old Testament are referred to or represented in the finds several times. We have a complete copy of Habakkuk and we have another copy of Isaiah, which is very important for checking with the other copy as well. It is only one-third, but it is more or less complete from chapter forty-one to the end.

All of this is tremendously exciting and even now has not been fully explored and unravelled. The Dead Sea Scrolls constitute another independent witness to the substantial reliability of the text we have. They do deviate, and there are some very interesting deviations from the text we have, but in substance they confirm the absolute reliability of the Masoretic Text. That in itself is exciting. Of course it takes our whole study of the text to nine hundred years earlier at least. That is rather wonderful.

## The Septuagint

The third means of checking the Masoretic Text is what we call the Septuagint. It is the Latin word for "seventy" and often it is written in Roman numerals—LXX—that is the way you can understand the Septuagint. This is the oldest version of the whole Old Testament, being a translation into Greek made in Alexandra in the third century before Christ. It was probably completed by the end of the second century before Christ. Now again this is important. It was for the benefit of Greek-speaking Jews who lived all around the Mediterranean and were not Aramaic speaking people living in Palestine and Syria. It was supposed to have been made by seventy-two elders sent down from the Holy Land to Egypt in seventy-two days in seventy-two separate cells. Hence it was called the Septuagint. They forgot the two and just called it the seventy. It is generally considered to be "fearful Greek." One scholar has called it Hebrew in disguise. Its great value lies in its being an independent check on the Masoretic Text for it embodies a basic text other than the Masoretic. It varies in different places—in Samuel, Kings, Job, and elsewhere, but especially in Samuel and Kings it varies quite a lot. However, it essentially substantiates the Masoretic Text.

Sometimes the Septuagint corrects our Masoretic Text where copyists have gone astray and there has been an obscuring of the original meaning. Thus in your margin you will sometimes see "Hebrew corrupt." The Septuagint gives us the key to what was originally there, but more often, and this we must stress, the Masoretic Text proves its superiority. Of course, the Septuagint was the version of the Old Testament used by the early church. They did not use the Hebrew because most of them did not speak Hebrew. They spoke Greek, so naturally they used the Septuagint. That is why in your New Testament you will find that often the quotation of the Old Testament is a little different from what you find in your Old Testament because they are quoting the Septuagint Version and not the Hebrew. The best and earliest manuscripts of the Septuagint date from the fourth and fifth century after Christ, some four centuries earlier than the known Masoretic manuscripts.

## The Syriac Version/The Peshitta

We have a fourth means of checking the Masoretic Text, and it is what we call the Syriac Version, which probably many people have never heard of. The Syriac Version is called the Peshitta.

This version of the Old Testament was in Syriac, and it was a translation from Hebrew, made probably in the second or third century AD. It was revised, unfortunately, a century or two later in the light of the Septuagint. Therefore, it is not so valuable a check as it would have been if it had been left independent of the Septuagint. Nevertheless, it is another witness added to the others for the reliability of our text. The earliest full manuscripts of the Peshitta date from the sixth or seventh century AD.

## The Latin Vulgate

The fifth means of checking the Masoretic Text is what we call the Latin Vulgate. This is a translation of the whole Bible into Latin. In fact, the New Testament was more of a revision because there were already old Latin copies of the New Testament. It was made by Jerome who was the greatest scholar amongst the early church fathers and the man who would not suffer fools when he came to writing his Latin Version. He got into a lot of trouble with traditionalists who as always did not like their favourite text tampered with even if it was more authentic and genuine. I am afraid there is a letter extant in which he calls them two-legged asses. He obviously did not put up with fools easily even if they were Christians. He was the greatest scholar amongst the church fathers and he made this translation about 400 AD; the usual date is 382 AD.

Why do we mention him particularly? It is because his New Testament was a revision of the existing Latin in the light of Greek, but his Old Testament was a translation from Hebrew. Therefore, in the Latin Vulgate we have a translation of the text some 500 years earlier than our extant manuscripts, and this in itself is again a check. Of course, people who are Latin scholars have got to think back as to how the Latin would have sounded in Hebrew. It is not an easy job, but nevertheless with the other versions it proves an added check upon the Masoretic Text.

What is generally agreed to by all scholars is that the Masoretic Text upon which our Old Testament is based is superior to all the others. There are one or two voices raised against it, but generally speaking, it is a unanimous and universal verdict. It is looked upon as not only being superior to the others but as being more reliable, more trustworthy, and more accurate.

Let me quote something that Professor F.F. Bruce, one of the foremost authorities on the text, said in his book, *Second Thoughts on the Dead Sea Scrolls*:

> *But in general, the new discoveries have increased our respect for the Masoretic Hebrew text. In a number of places it calls for emendation, but over the whole area of the Old Testament writings, its superiority to the other forms of text current at the end of the pre-Christian era is assured. The great, 'indeed the all-important question' which Sir Frederic Kenyon asked in 1939 is well on the way to receiving a much more explicit and positive answer than was thought possible then: 'Does this Hebrew text, which we call Masoretic, and which we have shown to descend from a text drawn up about A.D. 100, faithfully represent the Hebrew text as originally written by the authors of the Old Testament books?'*

# Versions that Help with Clarity

These versions we have mentioned—the Peshitta, the Septuagint, and the Latin Vulgate—help us in determining the meaning of a verse which has become corrupted or seems obscure. We will look at some abbreviations that are used in some of the versions. For some reason the Revised Version and the American Standard Version decided not to use these abbreviations in their footnotes or they use them very sparingly if at all. But the Revised Standard Version of the Old Testament decided to use these abbreviations. As you read your Old Testament, if you look down at your footnotes and you see *gk* you will know that is a reference to the Septuagint. If you see *syr* you will know it is a reference to the Peshitta, or the Syriac Version. If you see *sam* you will know it is a reference to the Samaritan Pentateuch. If you see *vg* you know it is a reference to the Latin Vulgate. If you see *cm* you will know it means correction.

We will look at four examples beginning with Zechariah 13:6 and the phrase: "What are these wounds in thine hands?" You will notice that in the Revised Version and the American Standard Version we have this: "What are these wounds between thine arms?" There is a reference, which Monsignor Knox points out very clearly and rather pointedly, in II Kings where the Hebrew does speak of a wound from an arrow being shot through him "between his arms," but that is not the same here.

In the Revised Standard Version you will see, "What are these wounds on your back?" It makes no particular reference in the footnote. The Authorised Version (KJV) says, "What are these wounds in thine hands?" The Revised Version and the American

Standard Version says, "What are these wounds between your arms?" The Revised Standard Version says, "What are these wounds on your back?" What are we to make of it?

If we turn to the Syriac Version, which is an independent version of the Masoretic Text, it says: "And they shall say to him, what are these wounds in your hands?" In the Septuagint, Zechariah 13:6, we find this: "What are these wounds between your hands?" They have literally translated the Hebrew. This is very important because it shows us that evidently the original Hebrew was something like this "between your hands."

The Latin Vulgate says, "Ask they, what wounds be these in thy clasped hands?" You see, between thy hands. Now Knox puts an interesting footnote in here. He says, "literally 'between thy hands', a difficult phrase most inadequately interpreted by some moderns as meaning 'on thy back.' If the sacred author had meant 'between thy arms,' he would surely have said so, as in II Kings 9:24."

If you look up those versions it seems clear we have a clear messianic prediction of the sufferings of the Lord Jesus Christ. It seems as if we have got it there.

Let's look at another text in Isaiah 53:10. This is the very famous reference in that wonderful chapter about the Lord Jesus: "When thou shalt make his soul an offering for sin." The Authorised Version (KJV), the Revised Version, and the American Standard Version all give the rendering: "When thou shalt make his soul an offering for sin," although the Revised Version and the American Standard Version give the alternative in the margin. The Revised Standard Version puts it this way: "When he makes himself an offering for sin," not so much a prediction of when you and I will take the sacrifice of Christ for our sin, but more of a prediction of his offering Himself on the cross for our sin. What are we to make of this? The Syriac, the Peshitta, puts it like this: "He laid down His life an offering for sin." That agrees with the Revised Standard Version. Again, Knox's translation of the Vulgate puts it like this: "His life laid down for guilt's atoning." Again we have some help. We have two clearly variant readings. In fact, it is the most wonderful thing because both are true. He did lay down His life as an offering for sin, and "When Thou shalt make His soul an offering for sin, He shall see His seed, He shall prolong His days." Both are absolutely true and here you have the versions that can help.

Let's turn to another very interesting reference in Genesis 4:8. Here is a really interesting example of corruption in the text. The Authorized Version says very awkwardly actually as far as the translation of Hebrew goes: "Cain talked with Abel." It is the best the translators of the 1611 version could make of it actually. The Revised Version and the American Standard Version put it like this: "Cain told his brother Abel." It is very interesting that the Syriac puts it like this: "Cain said to Abel, 'Let us go out into the field.'" The Septuagint agrees word for word. The Vulgate has this interesting variation: "Cain said to his brother Abel, 'Let us go out together.'" It is quite plain that something fell out of the original text. Why? Because of the next phrase, "And it came to pass when they were in the field." It is obvious. So the Revised Standard Version has put it in, and in the footnote you will see how to understand this. It says, "*H*, Samaritan, Greek, Syriac compare with the Vulgate. Hebrew lacks, 'Let us go out into the field.'" Now you have the idea. The new versions, where they feel there is an omission, are correcting it by these other very old versions. It is perfectly plain that when it said, "And Cain talked to his brother Abel, and it came to pass when they were in the field," it is obvious it should say, "Let us go into the field, and it came to pass when they were in the field that Cain slew his brother Abel."

Another interesting example is Exodus 17:16. Here, if you look at the footnote in the Revised Standard Version you will see it says, "Hebrew obscure." Then you have a little footnote, "correction *ca*." What is obscure? It is, in fact, rather obscure. The Authorised Version (KJV), the Revised Version, and the American Standard Version say, "The Lord has sworn," but you need to see the margin where even then they had some doubt about whether it should be translated, "The Lord has sworn." The Hebrew is literally, "a hand upon the throne of the Lord," and no one has been able to make a lot of sense of it. I do not know why. The Revised Standard Version has decided to correct it feeling that the Hebrew is corrupt and obscure, and has put: "a hand upon the banner of the Lord." I do not know whether that really is so good. The Septuagint puts it like this: "With a secret hand the Lord wages war upon Amalek for ever and ever." Isn't that lovely? That makes sense to me more than "the hand upon the banner." Knox's Vulgate puts it like this, and I am not so sure this is so good: "He cried, Lift up your hands to the Lord's throne." It is true because Moses had already lifted up his hands. "The Lord declares war against Amalek for ever and ever." Monsignor Knox adds a very interesting footnote here and his footnotes are good. "It is literally, in Latin, 'the hand of the throne of the Lord, and the war of the Lord, is against Amalek forever and ever.'" It agrees with the Septuagint: "a secret war, a secret hand is at war against Amalek." Now you see, these versions can be of help in determining obscurity in some verses. Sometimes these versions can throw more light upon the meaning of a verse.

A brother pointed out to me in the Latin Vulgate Version, Isaiah 53:4, the word "stricken, smitten of God, and afflicted" is put as "a leper, so we thought of Him smitten of God and afflicted." Of course, I thought to myself when the brother pointed it out to me what a strange thing. How did that word "leper" get into there? So the two of us made quite a little search in various versions, and we found that the Hebrew word for "stricken" can mean "plague." It is the word used in Leviticus where it is all to do with the plague of leprosy. It is the word used in Leviticus 13:2: "When a man shall have in the skin of his flesh a rising, or a scab, or a bright spot, and it becomes in the skin of his flesh the plague of leprosy." That is the word—"the plague of leprosy." There are an enormous number of instances of its use. So you can see that the old Latin Version is not so wild as we might think. When they translated this word, they evidently felt justified in translating it as "a leper." That was the idea behind it, and I have a feeling that it somehow implies more than stricken. It gives us more of the idea when we know what the Biblical meaning of leprosy is.

## The Ancient Manuscripts of the New Testament

What about the ancient manuscripts of the New Testament? The problem of establishing the correct New Testament text is comparatively easier than the Old Testament since we have a large number of Greek manuscripts preserving many variant forms of the original text. We have copies of the Greek New Testament written in the fourth century AD, quite substantial parts from the third century and some fragments from the second. The oldest fragment of one of the Gospels dates between 100 and 150 AD. In other words, as someone has said, "before the ink was almost dry upon the first manuscripts."

In all, there are manuscripts of all or part of the New Testament numbering more than four thousand. Thus, it can be seen that there has been a large amount of material through which we can determine the original New Testament text. Nevertheless, there is one sense at least, and I hope all those who are anti-Jewish will listen to me very carefully, in which determining the New Testament text is more difficult than the Old Testament. Some so-called Christian scribes seemed to have had no scruples whatsoever about adding, omitting, or changing what seemed to them best. This, the Jewish rabbis and scribes would never have dreamt of doing. In this sense, the problem of the New Testament text is more difficult than the Old Testament. Thus, sometimes because of heresies rapidly growing or for some other reasons, sometimes it was the person in the heresy, sometimes it was the orthodox, who were horrified by the heresy, or for some other reason, verses were made clearer or made more emphatic than in fact they were. Sometimes they were omitted because they did not quite back up the contention of the scribe or his party, or they were added in order to insert some authority for some particular thing. Now it is a good thing and a wonderful thing, it is marvellous in the hand of God that we have so many manuscripts extant by which we can judge what was the original New Testament text.

I am going to give you an example. The Authorised Version says in 1 John 5:6b–8: "It is the Spirit that beareth witness, because the Spirit is truth. For there are three that bear record in heaven, the Father, the Word, and the Holy Ghost: and these three are one."

The Authorized Version includes that in its text, but when you look in the Revised Version, the American Standard Version, the Revised Standard Version, the New English Bible, or the Syriac, every one of those omits this verse entirely, both in the text and the footnotes. Do you know the first time that verse ever appeared, as far as we know at present? The first time it appeared was in the writing of the Latin writer, Priscillian, in 385 AD, and thereafter we discover it in some old Latin manuscripts. It is not in a single one of our earliest and best Greek manuscripts. It is generally thought to have been inserted at the time when the heresy was growing rapidly which denied the deity of our Lord Jesus Christ. So we have this insertion "the Father, the Word, and the Holy Ghost." But is that so? Monsignor Knox again has a very interesting footnote on this. The Latin Vulgate does not include it either. It is unknown to all the early versions as well as the manuscripts. But Monsignor Knox puts this in a footnote: "The Latin manuscripts may have preserved the true text." That is why in all of the revised versions and all the modern versions that verse does not appear. It is not considered to even have a claim to go into the footnote. So it is expunged altogether from the record.

In the light of this, it needs to be emphasized that we have more evidence for the original text of the New Testament than any other work which has come down to us from the ancient world. I am going to quote Bishop Westcott in the book that he wrote called *Some Lessons from the Revised Version*:

*The popular interest felt in a few well-known variations, particularly in the omission of some familiar passages, has, no doubt, produced an exaggerated impression of the importance of the textual changes. It cannot therefore be repeated too often that the text of the New Testament surpasses all other Greek texts in the antiquity, variety and fulness of the evidence by which it is attested. About seven-eighths of the words used are raised above all doubt by a unique combination of authorities; and of the questions which affect the remaining one-eighth a great part are simply questions of order and form, and such that serious doubt does not appear to touch more than one-sixtieth part of the whole text.*

I would like to read to you something that I think is tremendous. It is from the preface of the Revised Standard Version of 1946:

*We now possess many more ancient manuscripts of the New Testament and are far better equipped to seek to recover the original wording of the Greek text. The evidence for the text of the books of the New Testament is better than for any other ancient book, both in the number of extant manuscripts and in the nearness of the date of some of these manuscripts to the date when the book was originally written.*

## The Most Important Manuscripts for the New Testament

Now the most important manuscripts we have for the New Testament come from between the fourth and the sixth century

AD. Amongst them are these three: the Codex Sinaiticus, the Codex Vaticanus, and the Codex Alexandrinus. These three are among the most important of the manuscripts we have. The Codex Sinaiticus dates from the fourth century and it is of the whole Bible and is now in the British Museum, parts of the Old Testament are missing.

The Codex Vaticanus dates approximately from the same time as the Codex Sinaiticus. It is missing Hebrews 9:14 to the end, the pastoral letters, Philemon, and Revelation. That resides in the Vatican library as you can imagine from its name. The Codex Alexandrinus dates from the fifth century and it is also in the British museum.

Scholars today tend to divide all this material I have mentioned, 4,000 extant manuscripts, into five basic families. In the Old Testament there are three basic families, but in the New Testament there are roughly five basic families. These basic families, each one representing the original text, are not independent of one another. They, in fact, do rely on and borrow a certain amount from one another. These five are the Byzantine, the Alexandrian, the Western, the Ceasarean, and the Antiochian.

The Byzantine is known often as the Received Text, and it underlies the Authorized Version. It is based on the Codex Alexandrinus, and it dates roughly from the fourth century.

The Alexandrian, sometimes called the Neutral text, is thought often to be nearest to the original text and it underlies the Revised Version and the American Standard Version. That is why there is a difference between the Authorised Version (KJV) and the revision.

The Western text dates from the second century AD and it is the text of the old Latin versions. More recently scholars have felt this is nearer to the original than was first thought. It is not later than 150 AD.

The Ceasarean is the one that is not easy to determine. It would seem, many think, to be a correction of the Western in the light of the Alexandrian.

The Antiochian is the basis of the Old Syriac Version. Again, it cannot be later than 150 AD.

## Additional Ways of Checking the Original Text

Are there any other ways of checking on the original text to the New Testament? There are two main ways. The first, again, are the early versions of the New Testament and the most important of these are the Latin, the Syriac, and the Coptic, dating from the second and third century AD. The other means of checking on the original text of the New Testament is from quotations of the New Testament in early writers, principally Greek, Syriac, and Latin from the second to the fourth century AD.

Our latest versions, especially the Revised Standard Version and the New English Bible, and so on, are based on all these, each variant reading being considered on its merits and no one particular family of these five being favoured. Now the Authorised Version (KJV) favoured the Byzantine; the Revised Version, and the American Standard Version the Alexandrian. However, the Revised Standard Version takes them all in, and so does the New English Bible. Thus, we can say a little more perhaps about the English Authorized Version of 1611. This was based on the Received Text, derived by Erasmus from a few late manuscripts and published at Basel in 1516. The most important manuscripts, the Sinaiticus and Vaticanus and others had not even been discovered at that time. So it was only natural that he published his Greek New Testament text in the light of what was known which was the Alexandrinus and it was based on the Byzantine text. This edition of the Greek text was substantially the Byzantine text and it included a comparatively small number of verses or phrases and one passage not represented in the earliest and most reliable manuscripts. Thus, the Revised Version, the American Standard Version, the Revised Standard Version, and the New English Bible omit these altogether, or relegate them to footnotes. That explains why some well-known passages, at least those you know well, have been put into the footnotes. They are relegated to the footnotes rather than omitting them altogether if there is some possibility of their representing the true, original text.

We will look at one or two. We have already looked at 1 John 5:7, and I just give it again as an example of a verse omitted altogether by all modern versions as not representing the original text.

Here is the biggest shock I suppose most of us would receive— John 7:53–8:11. This is the story of the woman taken in adultery. The Revised Version and the American Standard Version keep it in the text in brackets but they have the footnote: "most of the old manuscripts omit this passage." Those which contain it vary from each other. The Revised Standard Version places the whole passage in footnotes, rather awkwardly actually. The New English Bible places it on its own at the end of the Gospel of John and gives it its own little title: "An incident in the temple." It has completely removed it and put this footnote: "This passage, which in the most widely received editions of the New Testament is printed in the text of John 7:53 has no fixed place in our ancient witnesses." (They used the word witnesses for ancient versions and manuscripts.) Some of them do not contain it at all. Some place it after Luke 21:38, others after John 7:36, or John 7:52 or John 21:24. So you have that choice. I must say that whatever they all feel, inwardly, I have a strong intuitive feeling that that passage represents something absolutely authentic. It is very interesting that J. N. Darby has pointed out that in one manuscript the two pages have been torn out as if someone did not like it; it sort of seemed to speak of the Lord condoning immorality. Whether this is so or not we do not know. However, certainly it is authentic and it is interesting that in all the versions they have not omitted it altogether. They have placed it elsewhere because they are not at all certain, with a lot of justification, that it belongs to that particular position in John, after the 52nd verse of chapter 7.

Let's look at John 5:3–4, and again you know this is about the moving of the water. It says that an angel used to go down at certain times and whoever got in first after that was healed. Now in your Revised Version, the American Standard Version, the Revised Standard Version, and the New English Bible it has been placed in the footnotes. In other words, they felt they could not omit it altogether because it may well represent the original, but all the earliest manuscripts do not include it in its Authorised Version (KJV) place.

Then again a portion that I am very fond of is Acts 8:37. I will never forget when I first found it relegated to the footnotes, I nearly wept. The Revised Version, the American Standard Version, the Revised Standard Version, the New English Bible, all place this in the footnotes. This is where Philip, speaking to the eunuch said, "If thou believest with all thy heart, thou mayest." And he answered and said, "I believe that Jesus Christ is the Son of God." That is beautiful. It is not in the earliest, but it is a very interesting addition. This is the point that has interested many scholars, because it undoubtedly embodies the very simple question asked before people were baptized and the answer that was given before they were publicly baptized.

I have only given you four points to think about, of course there are a number of others. Sometimes the various versions will help us to understand what is meant. I am going to give you just one little instance of this which has been a blessing to me in Revelation 21:6. The Authorised Version (KJV) puts this: "It is done. I am Alpha and Omega, the beginning and the end." The Revised Version, and the American Standard Version put it like this, and I am rather sad about it, "They are come to pass." I do not see what sense that makes. When I read it in my Standard Version, which I use more than any other, I thought, What does that mean, "They are come to pass"? It has not come to pass. The New English Bible puts it: "They are already fulfilled." Does it mean that everything in this book is already fulfilled or already fulfilled in the mind of God? What does it mean? I am very interested that the Revised Standard Version has gone back to the Authorised Version (KJV) rendering and has put: "It is done." Well done, I say. "It is done." I am even more interested to read this, which I think is the most beautiful rendering of all in the Vulgate, and I have a feeling it has the whole idea and puts it in a nutshell. The Vulgate puts it like this: "And he said to me, It is over." I love that. That to me is what it really means. It is done; it is over. In other words, when it came to this final vision, the Lord Jesus was saying, "It is all over!" The whole thing has passed away, no more crying, no more death, no more mourning, no more suffering; it is over! Not, it is therefore fulfilled. It is over! That is the idea of it; it is finished! I am Alpha. I am Omega. I am the beginning; I am the end! I think that is just lovely.

## A Question of Punctuation

Then again there is another little interesting point in John 9, which a brother pointed out to me, and I think it is worth mentioning. In the American Standard Version, verses 3–4 it says: "Jesus answered, Neither did this man sin, nor his parents: but that the works of God should be made manifest in him. (Full stop) We must work the works of him that sent me, while it is day."

Here is a question of punctuation. The Authorised Version (KJV), the Revised Version, the American Standard Version, the New English Bible follow the same punctuation. Dr. Campbell Morgan, in one of his works, has queried this. He said, "I cannot help but feel that somehow or other there is something wrong with this verse. Surely it does not teach that a man could be paralyzed from birth just in order that God's work should be manifest in him." He was an Arminian, not a Calvinist and he was very, very upset indeed by the whole thing. He wrote to an eminent Greek scholar and asked: "Is there any reason why the punctuation should be like this? Why can't you remove the full stop after "in him" and read it like this: "Neither did this man sin nor his parents. (Full stop) But that the works of God should be made manifest in him, we must work the works of him that sent me while it is day." The scholar wrote back and said there is no reason at all why you should not do that. None of the versions do, but listen to this. Campbell Morgan did not know about this; I am afraid I have stumbled on it. This is the Peshitta and this is what it says. I think it is beautiful: "Jesus said to them, (Comma) neither did he sin nor his parents. (Full stop) But that the works of God might be seen in him, (Comma) I must do the works of him who sent me while it is day." Does that in fact embody the true meaning of that verse?

Again, there is another very interesting little query about punctuation in Romans 9:5. This is a very important one actually. We read: "Whose are the fathers, and of whom is Christ as concerning the flesh, (Comma) who is over all, God blessed for ever." This is a wonderful declaration of the divinity and deity of the Lord Jesus. "Who is God over all, blessed for ever." The Authorised Version (KJV), Revised Version, and American Standard Version give that punctuation. Our Revised Standard Version and the New English Bible give another. This is what they say for Romans 9:5: "To them belong the patriarchs and of their race, according to the flesh, (Comma) is the Christ. (Full stop) God who is over all, be blessed forever." It doesn't mean the same.

When we look at the Vulgate, there is a most emphatic rendering of this in favour of the former. It puts it like this: "The patriarchs belong to them and theirs is the human stock from which Christ came. Christ, (Comma) who rules as God over all things, blessed forever. Amen." That could not be more definite.

The Syriac Version, it is worthy of note, puts it like this: "And the fathers from among whom Christ appeared in the flesh who is God over all to whom are due praises and thanksgiving for ever and ever. Amen." So there is some help that we can get from these various versions.

## In Conclusion

I will summarize this in conclusion. When one remembers the 4400 years of copying by hand, the complexity of many of the records, the amount of material involved, the generally unscientific way, to us now in the twentieth century, in which these things were approached and handled, the human factors of failure, weakness, and inefficiency, the ravages of time and war, the perishable nature of the materials used in writing, the desire of heresies to conform the text to their own convictions, and sometimes the equally great desire of orthodoxy to rule out any embarrassing Scriptures they came across, it is a miracle of no small degree that we have so few real points of variation in the text. In fact it is singularly remarkable, considering all the evidence we have, that we hold today in our hands a text, both of the Old Testament and of the New Testament, which is substantially and essentially what was originally written, and to whose accuracy all the latest discoveries testify. When we bring all the points of doubt we have in the text, due to any mistake in copying or human failing, and place them together, we discover that no major or minor theme of the Bible is impaired or injured at all, and not one single doctrine of the whole of Scripture is affected, not even by the accumulation of all the so-called mistakes.

All this cannot be explained other than by the sovereign oversight of God in a most amazing way. We have in this volume a miracle, in my estimation, as great indeed, if not greater, than the very construction of the heavens, or of the design in life itself. Certainly it is a miracle more wonderful than any healing from disease that flabbergasts and amazes people so much, or even of raising someone from the dead. The presence of this Book today is an indication of the presence of God in history and human affairs. I do not think for a moment that you and I put the value upon this book that we ought. If someone was raised from the dead in our company, we would talk about it for years! If someone was healed, as well they could be and ought to be, we would talk about it again and again and again. Yet, in this volume we have a miracle, in my estimation, greater than all that and so remarkably evidenced in the way in which it has been finally brought to us. Indeed, as I said, in our study of the text of the Bible, we have enough evidence to try our faith and we have enough evidence to bring us to our knees in wondering trust. I do not think we can do any better than close the study on this particular subject than by quoting from a book by Sir Frederic Kenyon, one of the greatest authorities of the last century on textual criticism. He died just a few years ago. This is how he closed his little book called The *Story of the Bible*:

> It may be disturbing to some to part with the conception of
> a Bible handed down through the ages without alteration
> and in unchallenged authority; but it is a higher ideal
> to face the facts, to apply the best power for which God
> has endowed us to the solution of the problems which
> they present to us; and it is reassuring at the end to find
> that the general result of all these discoveries and all this

*study is to strengthen the proof of the authenticity of the Scriptures, and our conviction that we have in our hands, in substantial integrity, the veritable Word of God.*

# 3.
# The History of the English Bible

I think it is true to say that in the whole of human history no book has been translated more times than the Bible. Beginning with the main ancient translations, there were a number of Greek versions in the centuries immediately before Christ was born, and they resolved themselves into the official version that we now call the Septuagint Version. Another one of the ancient versions was the Syriac Version of the Bible that we call the Peshitta. This is another very old version and was a translation into Syriac in the early centuries of the Christian era. Then of course there are the old Latin Versions, which finally resolved themselves into what we call the Latin Vulgate. The word *vulgate* means "popular" or "common." It was Jerome's Version in 382 AD that came to be called the Vulgate and later on was finally and officially recognized by the Roman Catholic Church as their official version, to this day, of the Scriptures. Of course, it is the Latin Vulgate that is important to us for this time, not so much the Greek Version or the Syriac Version. It was the Latin Vulgate that became the basis for any translation, in part or whole, of the Bible in Europe, in whatever part of Europe it was.

These three main ancient translations of the Bible grew very quickly in number in the early centuries of this era. There are many very interesting versions that we are not going to talk about at this time. There are a number of Coptic Versions in different Coptic dialects, which are very interesting. These are from the ancient Christians of Egypt. There is a Georgian Version which is a very ancient translation. There is also an Armenian translation, an Ethiopic translation, a Slovanic translation, and a Gothic translation. All these different ones belong to the early centuries of this era.

When Luther translated the Bible into German in the 16th century, he had some fifteen translations in front of him, which he compared when he made his historic translation. By 1600 there were forty translations. By 1700 there were fifty-two translations. By 1938 there were one thousand translations of the Bible, and by 1958 there were 1,100 translations of the entire Bible—not fragments but the entire Bible. There is a particularly interesting book called *The Book of a Thousand Tongues*, which gives samples of all the thousand translations of the Bible in 1938. Then there is a book by the Wycliffe translators which also gives a rather interesting little selection of modern and old translations of the verse: "Go ye into all the world and make disciples of all nations" (Matthew 28:19). The number is still growing and it is an amazing fact that rapidly now, more and more languages are being used to bring God's Word to people.

Why do we speak about this question of translations? Well, our own English Bible is a translation and sometimes

English Christians forget that. You may remember the story of the old lady who, when she heard the minister reading from the Revised Version, was exceedingly indignant and stormed up to him afterwards to berate him for using the Revised Version. When he said that the Revised Version was very accurate, her retort was that the Authorised Version (KJV) was good enough for St. Paul and it was good enough for her!

It is true that there are still a number of English Christians who seem to think that the Authorised Version (KJV) was in fact the original that was in Paul's hand. It was sort of the language he wrote. In fact, our English Bible is a translation, and that is why we are talking about translations.

## God's Sovereign Oversight

Sometimes some of the languages used for translating the Bible presented very real difficulties indeed. For example, how do you describe a palm tree to an Eskimo? In fact, how do you speak of a desert to an Eskimo? How do you speak of a crocodile or a pomegranate? These things are not so silly as you may think. Crocodiles are only mentioned once or twice, but pomegranates figure quite a bit in certain parts of the Bible. These are the kind of difficulties that have been presented to translators of the Bible. Our own English translators had a lot of difficulty botanically, as I think some botanists here will probably point out. In the end they just gave up and instead of trying to give us what they knew in some cases to be the correct word, they simply settled on some well-known English flower or tree or fruit and translated it as such. This, in fact, has had to happen in a number of languages.

For instance, the Eskimo does not know what a lamb is, and therefore the whole teaching of the Bible from beginning to end about the Lamb of God has no meaning to him at all. So the translators, after much prayer translating the Eskimo version of the Scriptures, have called the Lord Jesus 'the seal pup of God,' and that means everything to the Eskimo. He understands quite clearly what a seal pup is and it makes sense.

It is another remarkable evidence of God's sovereign oversight concerning this volume that we call the Bible, that its entire contents have been put faithfully into the language of the people all over this globe. It is a remarkable fact when you think of some of the portions in Ephesians, and Colossians, and Romans, and Hebrews that have been faithfully put into the languages of people that they can understand, all over this world. It is no mean feat to have done this. It is an evidence of the oversight of God in bringing this Book in its entirety to the peoples of the world. It is a very wonderful thing that John said, prophetically, that in the end, of all nations, and kindreds, and tongues and peoples there should come a great enumerable redeemed multitude. He little realised I think, just at that time, how the very book he himself was in the process of writing was going to be put into every tongue that the world knows.

## Chapter and Verse Divisions

Another point we ought to make before we look at the history of our English Bible is that neither chapter nor verse divisions were any part of the original. Again, this is another point which many Christians overlook. They think that the prophets actually marked off the chapters and probably marked off the verses as well, and that both chapters and verses are as inspired as the text. This, of course, is very wide of the mark altogether. When these messages were given, there were no chapters. Even when they were written down, there were no chapters or verses at all. They were written, as we know, a book of rather lengthier divisions. In fact, the division into verses that we have can be traced to the early centuries of this era. The Masoretes fixed the verse division of the Old Testament in the year 900 AD. That is very late, and it divides the Old Testament into exactly 23,100 verses. The division into chapters was much later and was the work of a cardinal in the 13th century. Both the chapter and the verse divisions together first appeared in what we call Bomberg's Great Bible of 1547–1548. That was the first time the chapters and verses that you and I know appeared in the Bible together.

The first English Bible that had both chapter and verse divisions that we know was the Geneva Bible of 1560. Before that, some of them had chapter divisions, but none of them had verse divisions. Some scholars of the Revised Version and the modern versions have felt it to be a scourge. The verses and chapters that you and I know were no part, in fact, of the original.

## The First Scriptures in the English Language

What can we say about the actual history of the English Bible? First, right back in the beginning, the Latin Vulgate of Jerome was a very fine translation of the Bible into Latin. Jerome was a very fine scholar. Indeed, he was the outstanding scholar amongst the church fathers.

We have to jump over quite a period of time before we come to the first occurrence of the scriptures in the language of the English or British people. It was in the eighth century, the 700s roughly, that we find the first actual occurrences of English Scripture. It began with a gentleman called Caedmon who was a laborer in a monastery in the north of England. He was asked to go to a party, so the story goes, and he was frightened to death that he would be asked to sing at the party for fun. So he went and hid himself in a barn, and there he fell asleep. While he was asleep an angel came to him and told him to sing, so he began to sing. When he sang in his vision or dream, he began to sing a story about the creation of the world. Now, this man could neither read nor write. When he woke up, what he had sung, both the ballad form of the words and the tune, were in his mind. After that he began to sing and caused quite a sensation, quite as great as any pop singer today, I might say. People from all over the place began to come and listen to Caedmon singing the scriptures, for without ever having read the scripture, he began to sing the stories of the Bible in ballad form.

Now the lady who was in charge of this monastery and convent, an abbess, was a lady called Hilda. She was most interested in Caedmon and asked him to become a monk. She felt that God had gifted him, very definitely (by the way these are early Christians and true believers and not just nominal Christians) so she asked him if he would join her staff. He did, and she and other of the inmates began to teach him what the Bible said. They began to translate from the Latin to the English and put it into his mind. He in turn put it into ballad form and began to sing it. We believe this, in fact, was the beginning of the English Bible. For the first time, as far as we know, the Bible was beginning to be spoken, in a paraphrase form, in the language of the people.

In about 700 AD there is a version of the Psalms by Aldhelm, bishop of Sherborne. Then, I suppose we have all heard of the Venerable Bede. He is accredited with a translation of the Gospel of John, and he died almost on the last word of translation. After that there are a number of other fragments that belong to this era.

Then King Alfred, who I suppose you know as the one who burnt the cakes, was in fact far more famous for his very enlightened government. He was a man who loved the Lord and he was immersed in his Bible. He prefixed to the laws of the realm the Ten Commandments, which he himself translated out of the Latin Vulgate into English as it was then spoken. He also translated those chapters of Exodus 21–23 that later on the Puritans were to call "The Book of the Covenant." So it is rather remarkable really that those are the first examples we have of the Bible in English.

In the Norman era, after 1066, these translations came to an end for the simple fact that the Normans were French and all the ruling and educated classes spoke, wrote, and read French. The result was there was no more translation of the Bible into the language of the common people. It was in the 14th century that more English versions appeared. They were versions of the Psalms, the book of Revelation, Paul's letters, Acts, and what we call the general letters—James, Jude, Peter, and so on.

# The First Great Milestone in the Story of the English Bible

All these led up to the most important date, the first real milestone in the story of the English Bible, which was John Wycliffe's version of the Bible in 1388. In fact, this was the first complete translation of the entire Bible into English, but it was from the Latin Vulgate. Wycliffe, who I think most of you will remember from your history lessons at school, was one of the most remarkable and enlightened men of his day. He was the leader of a large group that has come to be called Lollards. They were God's people, and they were nicknamed the Lollards.

Wycliffe had one great passion and that was to put the Bible into the language of the people. He took the Latin Vulgate and translated it into English. We can call it the pioneer version of the English Bible even though it was a translation of a translation.

There were, in fact, two Wycliffite Versions of the Bible, neither being the work personally of Wycliffe himself. He was the inspirer of both versions, but he did not personally translate these versions. The first was produced in his lifetime in 1384, and it was a very literal translation of the Latin Vulgate. It was so literal that it kept the Latin order and even used Latinised English. Therefore, it did not have the popular appeal that it should have had. The second appeared in 1388, after Wycliffe had died. It was a very careful revision of the first, made by John Purvey who was Wycliffe's secretary. It was made in a much more natural English. In fact, it was the natural English spoken by the common people. This was an absolute milestone in the story of the Bible. For the first time now, the people had the entire Bible in their own language.

John Purvey was a remarkable man. He was a most delightful man, shown especially in the preface that he wrote to the 1388 edition of Wycliffe's Bible, where he calls himself in one place a "poor scribbler."  In another place he refers to himself as that "coward sinful caitiff." He was a most humble man with no feeling about his own reputation as a translator. In fact, he was no mean translator; for we believe it is to him that we owe the "englishing" of the Wycliffe Bible.

The whole work was regarded with grave suspicion by many people in high places in the Country and bitterly opposed by the church. In the House of Lords a bill was introduced immediately to try and suppress this version of the Bible, but John of Gaunt stood up, and through his influence, the bill was rejected and the people continued to have the Bible in their own language.

In 1408, however, the church ruled that no one, *no one* should translate any text of Scripture whatsoever into English, nor should any such be read publicly or privately by anyone on pain of excommunication. Of course, excommunication did not just mean you were put outside of the church and you could go on with everything else. It meant everything. You lost your job. You lost your reputation. You lost your means of livelihood. Everything was gone from you. This led to the most terrible persecution. This is not in the course of the story, but if you want to you can read *Foxe's Book of Martyrs* and other books of the history of the church in England. It was in this period that so many people were burned at the stake simply because they were discovered reading the Bible in English. For no other reason many of them were burned at the stake that "their spirit may be saved though their body be destroyed." That was Roman Catholic teaching at that time. Nevertheless, thank God, the initial breakthrough had taken place and things would never be the same again for this country. For the first time the Bible had been put into English and the people had begun to read it, and nothing now could stop the onward move of the English Bible.

## The Tyndale Bible—The Next Great Milestone

The next great milestone in the story of the English Bible is William Tyndale's Version of the New Testament. This was the first printed edition of the New Testament in English, and it appeared in 1525. Up to this point, all copies of the Bible whatever they were—Latin or English— had to be copied by hand. This was the first printed version ever to be made. It was also the first translation ever to be made from the Greek original. So this version of William Tyndale's marks another great milestone in the story of the English Bible. Printing had been invented and this was going to be the means by which God's Words could be disseminated throughout the nation and indeed throughout the world. Secondly, someone now was not making a translation of a translation, but was going right back as far as he could to the original text of God's Word, and putting it into the language of the people. This was a major breakthrough for God and for the interest of His kingdom. He, of course, translated it from the Greek text in the light of the Latin Vulgate and in the light of Luther's German translation. It was bitterly opposed by the church. Tunstall, bishop of London, who I am quite sure will not be discovered in heaven, bought up the whole first edition and publicly burned it at St. Paul's Cross. This only inflamed the people's appetite to read this forbidden book all the more. Secondly, it provided William Tyndale with a large sum of money with which to produce a much larger edition. In fact, here is a very amusing and contemporary true account of what happened, written by the gentleman who was in the deal.

> *The Bishop, thinking he had God by the toe, when indeed he had, (as after he thought) the devil by the fist, said, "Gentle Master Packington," (who was a merchant and was in fact dealing with these Scriptures, this edition of the New Testament), "Do your diligence and get them, and with all my heart I will pay for them, whatsoever they cost you, for the books are erroneous and naughty, and I intend surely to destroy them all and to burn them at Paul's Cross."*

> *Augustine Packington came to William Tyndale and said, "William, I know thou art a poor man, and hast a heap of New Testaments and books by thee for the which thou hast both endangered thy friends and beggared thyself, and I have now gotten thee a merchant which with ready money shall dispatch thee of all that thou hast, if you think it so profitable for yourself."*

> *"Who is the merchant?" said Tyndale.*
> *"The Bishop of London," said Packington.*
> *"Oh, that is because he will burn them," said Tyndale.*
> *"Yea, Mary," quoth Packington.*
> *"I am the gladder," said Tyndale, "for these two benefits shall come thereof. I shall get money of him for these books to bring myself out of debt, and the whole world shall cry out upon*

*the burning of God's Word." (He was a very wise man.) "And*
*the overplus of the money, that shall remain to me, shall*
*make me more studious to correct the said New Testament,*
*and so newly to imprint the same once again, and I trust*
*the second will much better like you, than ever did the first."*
*And so forward went the bargain. The bishop had the books,*
*Packington had the thanks, and Tyndale had the money.*

That is a contemporary version of what exactly happened. They were not without their humour in those days.

Tyndale was in fact, a most remarkable Christian. His supreme passion was to place God's Word in the hands of the ordinary man in his own language. Perhaps, even he little realised the power and the influence such a course of action was to have. In many ways, spiritually, it was like the first atom bomb that was dropped at Hiroshima; it ushered in a new era. I wonder sometimes whether Tyndale realised it. He was once very angered in a discussion he had at a certain place by someone who said that he thought the pope's laws were far more important than God's laws. Tyndale was so angry that in a moment of anger he retorted: "Before long I mean to see that every boy that driveth a plough shall know more about God's Word than you do."

Well, he did not actually live to see that fulfilled, but that is exactly what was to happen. For no other reason than his passion for putting God's Word into the language of the people, he was hounded all his life. He had to leave his home. He had to leave his livelihood; he was a very distinguished scholar. He had to leave Oxford and Cambridge and flee to the Continent where he lived most of his life in Germany and in the Lowlands. His whole life, if only you will read it, is one of the most moving stories in the annals of church history. He never was able to live comfortably for long. He was always on the move, always being spied upon, always being trapped. He had to watch every person. In his conversation he had to whisper. He was a man who really was martyred in spirit long before he was martyred in body.

His first edition of the English New Testament was printed in Germany, as also was the Pentateuch, which was printed in 1530, the first time that any translation had ever been made direct from the Hebrew text. In 1531 he printed the book of Jonah, again a direct translation from the Hebrew text, and he also translated other parts of the Old Testament. We are not absolutely sure how much he did translate, but they were translated from the Hebrew. He was martyred near Brussels in 1536, being first strangled and then burnt at the stake. Such was the price of the English Bible.

Yet in the last year, which he spent in prison, his life was so peerlessly beautiful and sincere that both his jailer and the jailer's daughter came to a saving knowledge of the Lord Jesus Christ. His last words before he was strangled were a prayer that the Lord would open the king of England's eyes.

Tyndale's simplicity, his freshness, and vitality have passed into the Authorised Version (KJV). His very fine sense of English style has provided, in fact, the standard for all succeeding versions. Of course, not all of his more idiomatic English passed into the Authorised Version. I might say, we can be quite glad about that. For instance, in Genesis 39:2, "The Lord was with Joseph and he was a lucky fellow." Again, he translated Exodus 15:4: "Pharaoh's captains" as "Pharaoh's jolly captains." Also in Exodus 15:26, he translated "the Lord that healeth thee," as "the Lord thy surgeon," possibly a good text we might need sometimes, but that is the way he did it. Those more quaint translations, which were not so quaint at that time, did not pass into the Authorised Version.

To him we owe some of the phrases that are embedded in all our spirits. For instance, this beautiful one: "Until the day dawn, and the daystar arise in your hearts" (II Peter 1:19). That was William Tyndale. Again, "In him we live and move and have our being" (Acts 17:28.) That is William Tyndale. Again that other beautiful sentence: "For here have we no continuing city but we seek one to come" (Hebrews 13:14). Also, strangely enough, the version of the Lord's prayer that we use, not the one we find in the Authorised Version (KJV) or in any succeeding version, but the version that we use in which we say, "Forgive us our trespasses, as we forgive them that trespass against us." That is William Tyndale's Version, not the Authorised Version of the Bible. So we owe a tremendous amount to William Tyndale who, with his own blood, actually paid the price for us to have the Bible in English.

I have often wondered why it is that the Bible in other nations was never sealed with blood as the English Bible was. I have come to the conclusion that the English Bible in Satan's mind was far more important than some of the other languages. He knew it was going to become the basis for much missionary translation and, in fact, was going to spread over a very large part of the world.

# The Coverdale Bible

The next great date in the story of the English Bible is in 1535. That is when the Coverdale Bible, the first printed edition of the entire Bible in English, was made. It was made by a man called Myles Coverdale, a companion and helper of Tyndale, and it was made from German and Latin because Myles Coverdale was not a Greek and Hebrew scholar. He quite honestly and sincerely pointed that fact out and made a translation from the Latin and the German translations in the light of Tyndale's existing manuscripts, as well as Luther and Zwingli and others. What was vastly important with the Coverdale Bible was the simple fact that Henry VIII relented and gave his royal permission. Tyndale probably never knew when he died that in fact an English Bible was circulating in these Islands, and when he prayed that God would open the King of England's eyes, before he had called, God had already started to answer. This was the first version in which the apocryphal books were separated from the canonical books and put on their own.

# The Matthew Bible

The next great date in the English Bible is 1537, two years later, and we call it the Matthew Bible or Matthew's Bible. This was the work of John Rogers, a companion and helper of Tyndale's. They were all associated together. In fact, both Coverdale and Rogers had to flee the country and for a while these godly men lived with and helped Tyndale in his work on the translation of the Bible.

Rogers assumed the name of Thomas Matthew for political expediency. It was not wise for him to use the name John Rogers. His edition would probably never have been allowed and may have aroused a lot of opposition, knowing that he was a great friend of Tyndale. So he assumed the scriptural name of Thomas Matthew and the book was a riotous success even in high quarters. It was a careful revision based on both Tyndale and Coverdale's translations going back to the two previous ones. In fact, in a lot of its parts it was Tyndale and Coverdale untouched. It is generally considered to be a very great improvement of both the preceding versions. This was the first Bible allowed by royal authority to be bought and read within the whole realm. That was different from just having permission that it might be translated into English and that the church officials and others who were educated might read it. It is an amazing fact to realise that within one year of Tyndale's death, his prayer had already been answered and two English versions of the entire Bible were circulating in Britain. That is an amazing fact!

John Rogers was finally burnt at the stake in 1555 during the reign of Queen Mary. He had eleven children and it is said that all eleven, including one babe in arms, went to watch him die at the stake. The story is told of him of his wonderful answers to Bishop Bonner, who again we shall not discover in heaven, and they are recorded in *Foxe's Book of Martyrs* and other histories. Perhaps the most remarkable story told of him at all is when the jailer's wife went to fetch him from the prison at Newgate the morning that he was to die, they found him soundly asleep as a little child. All the way down he embarrassed the church officials and others by singing Psalms right the way until finally he died at the stake.

Both Tyndale's Version and Matthew's Version had very controversial notes in the margin. When you read some of these notes, it is no small wonder that the reaction was so violent against them. For instance, in Exodus 32:35 we read, "The Lord plagued the people, because they made the calf, which Aaron made." In the margin of these Bibles was this note: "The pope's bull slayeth more people than ever did Aaron's calf."

Leviticus 21:5: "They shall not make baldness upon their head, neither shall they shave off the corner of their beard, nor make any cuttings in their flesh." The note in these Bibles in the margin is this: "Of heathen priests then, our prelates (or bishops) took example of their bold pates." These are only two examples of why such very great reaction was aroused against these dear men who in faithfulness really did stand out.

## The Great Bible

The next milestone in the story of the English Bible is 1539, and it is a very great milestone. We call it The Great Bible. It is called the Great Bible, not because it was in fact intrinsically greater than the others, but simply because of its size. It was a huge great Bible, especially printed to go in public places, particularly in churches. This again was the work of Myles Coverdale. He had a tremendous part to play, as you can see, in the story of the English Bible. It is basically a revision of Matthew's Bible. Archbishop Cranmer very kindly wrote a preface for the 1540 edition of this Bible. In 1541, no doubt partly due to his influence, by royal proclamation, for the first time a copy of the Bible in English was placed by law in every parish church in the realm of England. This was tremendous!

So now we have come step by step: first, royal permission. Secondly, people were allowed to buy and to read. Thirdly, by law it was placed in every parish church. In fact, they ran out of Bibles because they could not get enough to put in the parish churches, and they had to print edition after edition. It is also evident that the common folk enjoyed the Bible much more and found it much more interesting than the vicar. There was a royal proclamation made that people were not to read the Bible aloud in English during the services, and neither were they to discuss it. What was happening was so simple. People were sick to death of both their parsons and vicars because they could not understand anything they said. Most of the parsons and vicars were educated people and hardly ever bothered to try and speak in a way that the people could understand, and the people were so tired of them. During the service, they were much more interested to gather around where the Bible had been chained to its lectern. Someone who was literate read it out and they all discussed it and asked questions, much to the embarrassment of the vicar and the choir. By royal proclamation, people were told they were not allowed to disturb church services by reading the Bible or discussing it in English.

It was from this version, the Great Bible, that we have now today the Prayer Book Version of the Psalms. Some of you may have noticed, especially those of you with State Church backgrounds, that the Prayer Book Psalter differs from the Authorised Version (KJV) of the Psalms. That is because it is the Great Bible Version of Myles Coverdale. It was altered just a little.

In spite of the fact of some very quaint expressions in the Great Bible, Coverdale has influenced the Authorised Version (KJV) very, very greatly indeed. For instance, these are some of the Scriptures that have come to us from Coverdale. He was a master of rhythm: "Seek ye the Lord while he may be found, call ye upon him while he is near" (Isaiah 55:6). That is Coverdale's Version. "My flesh and my heart faileth: but God is the strength of my heart, and my portion for ever" (Psalm 73:26). That is Myles Coverdale; beautiful rhythm in his translation.

Some of the quainter expressions which never passed into the Authorised Version (KJV), I am sure we can be glad, are these. You know the phrase in Jeremiah 8:22: "Is there no balm in Gilead?" Coverdale translated it: "Is there no more treacle at Gilead?" Then in Psalm 91:5 where in the Authorised Version we read this: "Thou shalt not be afraid for the terror by night." Coverdale translated it: "Thou shalt not need to be afraid for any bugs by night." I am sure that could well be used in the East today. Actually, the word *bugs* then meant something quite different from what it does today. Also Psalm 45:5, which in fact we still have in our Prayer Book Version of the Psalms. "Good luck have thou with thine honour." Again in Zechariah 4:7: "He should bring up the first stone so that men shall cry unto him: 'Good luck, good luck,'" instead of they should cry: "Grace, grace unto it." You may well be glad that these quaint expressions have not come into our Authorised Version.

He also used the little exclamation that you get a lot of in Shakespeare—*tush*. He used it a lot. In fact, Professor Bruce says that he put it in many places where there was absolutely no reason at all to put it; for instance, the devil saying to Eve, "Tush, you shall not die." It comes again and again, but we can see straightaway that it is the language of the people and it meant something to them. It is quaint and does not mean anything to us, but it meant a lot to the people of his day.

## The Geneva Bible

The next milestone is the Geneva Bible of 1560. This is another great advance in the history of the English Bible. It is often called the Breeches Bible due to an unfortunate rendering in Genesis 3:7. "They sewed fig leaves together and made them aprons," was translated in this version as, "They sewed fig leaves together and made breeches." For some unaccountable reason it amused our forbearers no end; therefore they called the Geneva Bible the Breeches Bible.

The Geneva New Testament was published in the reign of Queen Mary; the complete Bible in 1560. It was a revision of the Great Bible and Tyndale's New Testament. So you can see that all these versions really go back on each other; they draw upon what precedes. This was in fact a revision of the Great Bible and William Tyndale's New Testament. Myles Coverdale had to flee the country and he was in Geneva where John Knox was, and where a man called William Whittingham was, and where Calvin and a number of other great reformers were gathered. Geneva, as it was then and has been all through the centuries, was a haven of refuge for believers. It so happened, under the sovereign oversight of God, that some of the greatest brains amongst the reformers were gathered, in exile really, in Geneva. Coverdale was one of them. He, with others who had sought refuge in Geneva, edited this version, added marginal notes, and for the first time, inserted words in italics to complete the sense of the original in English so that people reading might know it was not in the original but was inserted in order that we might understand the meaning. It was the first English Bible printed with verse and chapter divisions together. It was also the first English Bible printed in what we call Roman type. That is the type we are all used to today. It was the first step forward in that way.

The Geneva Bible was destined to become the most popular of all English versions to date. In fact, it became the household Bible of all English speaking Protestants. The Christians of this era loved the Geneva Bible, not only because it was scholarly, because it was accurate, because it was in beautiful English, but they loved the marginal notes. These notes were often highly controversial. (They were not so violent in some ways as some of the earlier ones, for which we can be thankful.) They were anti-papist; for instance in Revelation 11:7 which reads like this: "And when they shall have finished their testimony, the beast that ascendeth out of the bottomless pit shall make war against them, and shall overcome them, and kill them." The note they put in the margin was: "This is the pope which hath his power out of hell and cometh thence." It was a rather direct note I must say. It was beloved by all English speaking Protestants for its directness and frankness.

It was also anti-episcopal. It never translated the Greek by the word "bishop" but always as "elder." In many ways it was Presbyterian in character, as indeed were all the great reformed churches at that time of Switzerland, France, Scotland, a very large section of England, and of course the Lowlands in Holland. It was also highly Calvinistic. Therefore, these notes, highly Calvinistic, anti-bishop, anti-pope, made this version one of the most loved versions in English. Nevertheless, I think that even some of these notes were better than some that appeared before and since. I was horrified to see in the Barkley Version of 1959 a dreadful note next to Genesis 3:12 where Adam says to the Lord, "She made me to eat and I did eat." There in the margin of a modern version is this note: "Passing the buck is as old as humanity and shows no repentance." So you can understand that sometimes such notes are a bit disconcerting when you find them in the Bible. That is why the Authorised Version (KJV) translators tried to get rid of all such notes altogether, and I think with value.

There is another little note I would like to read to you so that you understand. I have quoted an anti-papal one, one which I think is rather crude. This I think is the choice of all notes in the Bible. This was in a Bible called Bishop Beck's Bible, which appeared just before the Geneva Bible in 1551 that never made a very great impression upon the English Bible. Perhaps it was just as well. Its notes, written by this Bishop Beck, were printed in exactly the same type as the text and almost became part of it. This is his note on 1 Peter 3:7 where men are exhorted to live with their wives according to knowledge. This bishop says in his notes: "He dwellth with his wife according to knowledge that taketh her as a necessary helper and not as a bondservant or a bondslave, and if she be not obedient and help flounder him, endeavoreth to beat the fear of God into her head that thereby she may be compelled to learn her duty and do it." Now you can understand perhaps why the Authorised Version (KJV) translators decided to get rid of all such notes.

## The Bishop's Bible

The next milestone or advance in the history of the English Bible was in 1568. We call it the Bishop's Bible. It was never very popular, although it was made the official version for England. It was the generally anti-bishop trend of the Geneva Bible and its rather controversial marginal notes that led to this version. It was produced by Anglican bishops and was a revision of the Great Bible. They were highly worried about the popularity of the Geneva Bible, and no wonder. It continued in use for some forty years, although the Geneva Bible was the most popular being almost universally read in private. So in spite of the fact that the bishops did their best to wipe out the Geneva Bible, it was read in the homes although the Bishop's Bible was read in church.

## The Douay Version of the Bible

The next version we ought to look at is not in a direct line, in one way, of the English Bible. It is the Douay Version of the Bible in 1609. In fact, it really stems from the translation of the Latin Vulgate and not of the Greek and Hebrew original. Nevertheless, it was rather important because it was the official Roman Catholic Version of the Bible in English. It was brought out, as its preface boldly states, to counteract the other English versions, which were making such headway amongst the people, not because it was felt that it was necessary for the people to read the Bible in their own language. In fact, it points out it thinks that is rather harmful. It was a translation as I have said of the Latin Vulgate, but it was done in the light of the Greek and Hebrew originals. I do not want to be amusing or facetious, but I must say it was, in fact, a very good thing for the Protestant cause that the Douay Version was so unreadable. It could have caused a counter reformation if it had really been in readable English. However, it was so Latinised that it never became popular, in fact in many cases it is quite hard reading the Douay Version. Some of the Latinisms are simply amazing. I will give you a few samples. For instance, how would you like this? Psalm 23:5: "… my cup runneth over." This is the Douay Version of 1609: "… my inebriating chalice, how goodly is it." Colossians 2:7 where we are told, "Rooted and built up in Him." We read in this version: "Rooted and super edified in Him." They were very fond of the word "super" by the way.

In Matthew 6:11, how would you like this for the Lord's Prayer? "Give us this day our super substantial bread." It referred for instance to our Lord where He speaks of Himself as the good Shepherd, as the good Pastor, because in Latin "pastor" is literally "shepherd." It was so Latinised that it was quite unbelievable, and it was a good thing for the Protestant cause that it was so unreadable. Many of the ordinary common people found it a highly amusing version. As they said in their preface that they did not feel it was so good for the people to read it, they had certainly produced a version that was not easy for the people to read. Its notes, as one would expect, were violently pro-Roman Catholic. Well, the Geneva Bible, Tyndale's Bible, and Matthew's Bible were in fact violently pro-Protestant, so we cannot grumble about that. Nevertheless, and this is a remarkable thing, the Douay Version has had influence on the Authorised Version (KJV). Do you know that we get our word "grace" from the Douay Version? We also get the word "advent" from the Douay Version in our Bible.

"Evangelise" is another word that comes from the Douay Version. These were not used before so much.

## The Authorised Version

Finally, we come to the Authorised Version (KJV) of 1611 where we shall finish. In 1604 at Hampton Court at a conference over which King James I presided, Dr. John Reynolds, a leader of the Puritan side in the Church of England, suggested that a new uniform translation of the Bible be made to cut out all these other versions which by then were existing alongside one another. It did not meet with the approval of the majority. In fact, some of the highest ecclesiastics were quite against it. However, what did matter is that it met with the approval of the King. This resulted in him appointing fifty-four men of learning and piety, of which forty-seven actually undertook the work in the end, to revise the existing translations of the English Bible. It was not really a translation, but a revision. There is a very interesting part in the preface. You very rarely find the preface now in the Authorised Version of the Bible. I have looked through all mine and I could not find it. But this is what the forty-seven translators of the Authorised Version put in their preface, which gives us the key to their version.

> Truly, good Christian reader, we never thought from the
> beginning, that we should need to make a new translation,
> nor yet to make of a bad one a good one; but to make a good
> one better, or out of many good ones, one principal good one,
> not justly to be excepted against. That hath been our endeavor,

*that our mark. To that purpose, there were many chosen that were greater in other men's eyes than in their own, and that sought the truth rather than their own praise. ... And in what sort did these assemble? In the trust of their own knowledge, or of their sharpness of wit, or deepness of judgment, as it were in an arm of flesh? At no hand. They trusted in him that hath the key of David, opening and no man shutting; they prayed to the Lord, the Father of our Lord, to the effect St. Augustine did: "O let thy Scriptures be my pure delight, let me not be deceived in them, neither let me deceive by them." In this confidence and with this devotion did they assemble together; not too many, lest one should trouble another, and yet many, lest many things haply might escape them.*

There is much else there, but that is enough for you to realise that their objective was to take all the preceding translations and out of them, in the light of the original Greek and Hebrew, to now make one principal one of many good ones. It was, in fact, the Bishop's Bible that was their immediate basis and then behind that they had the Geneva Bible, the Great Bible, Matthew's Bible and even Wycliffe's Version before them. To these they referred and gave very careful consideration in their translation. Thus the work of Wycliffe, of Tyndale, and Coverdale was before them. It has been estimated that sixty percent of the Authorised Version (KJV) text is taken from the earlier versions, the Geneva Bible and Tyndale's New Testament being the two principal sources. It resulted in a version which retained all of the best qualities of these preceding versions and yet somehow has produced a superlative style of its own. Thus came into being the version which was by its intrinsic merit to supersede all previous versions of the English Bible and to become the greatest single influence in the spiritual life of God's English speaking people.

When I was studying this afternoon, I realised with a shock that not one single great movement of God's Spirit over the years since the Authorised Version (KJV) did not use the Authorised Version, in the English speaking world, except possibly the Pentecostal movement which may have used the Revised Version. I do not think it has, in fact, but it may have. But every other movement of God's Spirit—the Quaker, the Puritan, the Wesleyan, and the Brethren has used the Authorised Version of the Bible. This was the Bible they loved. This was the Bible through whom they heard God speaking. It was in this Book, in this version that they began to have their eyes opened to see the Lord.

From even the purely secular angle, the Authorised Version (KJV) was destined to become the greatest single factor in English literature. You know, to me that is in some way thrilling. For when God does anything He does it perfectly. It seems that this Book has not only been able to contain the oracles of God and speak to us in a living way over the centuries, but it has also been in superlative English. It has been called the noblest monument to English prose. I do not think that there is any doubt surely, in any one of your minds, that it has ever been excelled by any version since. For its sheer beauty of style it stands supreme. It commended itself to all from its beginning. There was a certain amount of controversy at the very beginning as always, but in the end it commended itself to all because of the absence of any controversial notes and because of the absence of peculiarities. It is, in fact, quite remarkable.

I have not quoted quaint peculiarities just for a laugh, but because I want you to see that those peculiarities could have passed over into the Authorised Version (kjv) quite easily. However, in the most remarkable way, even now in the mid-twentieth century, there are very few quaint peculiarities in the Authorised Version. There are of course one or two, and the one I love best is in Galatians 1:11 where it reads: "And I certify you, brethren ..." I cannot think of anything funnier. I heard a vicar one evening reading solemnly from this: "I certify you, brethren." Of course, "I certify you, brethren," may have been quite different then to what it is now. It only means one thing now in that way, and that is a peculiarity. As a lad, I used to always love that other one about Paul coming to the Three Taverns and taking courage (see Acts 28:15). Apart from those two peculiarities in the Authorised Version, unless you know of others, I must say the Authorised Version is amazingly free from such quaint peculiarities. It is quite remarkable! Thus it became, in God's hands, the version that in many ways has become the foundation of all God has done in these others.

Next time we shall consider the Revised Version and all the new, modern versions that have come since the Authorised Version (kjv). We shall ask ourselves: Why is there a need for modern versions? I think we shall begin to see. When I said peculiarities, I did not mean that some words have not become obsolete or that there are not some incorrect translations in the Authorised Version, but what I mean is that it is not a laughable version. It is still absolutely dignified and it is still truly the Word of God in a style that somehow one feels is befitting.

I thought before we finish, I would end by reading a few selections from this version that I think will never be beaten.

First of all, of course, is Psalm 23. I noticed that even in the Revised Version and the American Standard Version they have wisely left it because it is absolutely perfect.

> *The Lord is my shepherd; I shall not want.*
> *He maketh me to lie down in green pastures: he leadeth me*
> *beside the still waters.*
> *He restoreth my soul: he leadeth me in the paths of*
> *righteousness for his name's sake.*
> *Yea, though I walk through the valley of the shadow of death,*
> *I will fear no evil: for thou art with me; thy rod and thy staff*
> *they comfort me.*
> *Thou preparest a table before me in the presence of mine*
> *enemies: thou anointest my head with oil; my cup runneth over.*
> *Surely goodness and mercy shall follow me all the days of*
> *my life; and I will dwell in the house of the Lord for ever.*

That cannot be beaten for absolute simplicity and rhythm.

Another random selection is in Isaiah 43:1–3, which is a different kind of translation, but it is still I think a perfect example of the "unbeatableness" of the Authorised Version (KJV) in some of its parts even to today.

> *But now thus saith the Lord that created thee, O Jacob, and he*
> *that formed thee, O Israel, Fear not: for I have redeemed thee, I*
> *have called thee by thy name; thou art mine.*
> *When thou passest through the waters, I will be with thee; and*

*through the rivers, they shall not overflow thee: when thou*
*walkest through the fire, thou shalt not be burned; neither shall*
*the flame kindle upon thee.*
*For I am the Lord thy God, the Holy One of Israel, thy Saviour.*

Then in Luke 15:11–24, although I know the modern versions, both the New English Bible and Phillip's Version are very racy and bring home the story, I do not think this rendering of the story will ever be beaten for simplicity and for effect in many ways.

*And he said, A certain man had two sons:*
*And the younger of them said to his father, Father, give me the*
*portion of goods that falleth to me. And he divided unto them*
*his living.*
*And not many days after the younger son gathered all together,*
*and took his journey into a far country, and there wasted his*
*substance with riotous living.*
*And when he had spent all, there arose a mighty famine in that*
*land; and he began to be in want.*
*And he went and joined himself to a citizen of that country;*
*and he sent him into his fields to feed swine.*
*And he would fain have filled his belly with the husks that the*
*swine did eat; and no man gave unto him.*
*And when he came to himself, he said, How many hired*
*servants of my father's have bread enough and to spare, and I*
*perish with hunger!*
*I will arise and go to my father, and will say unto him, Father, I*
*have sinned against heaven, and before thee,*
*And am no more worthy to be called thy son: make me as one*

*of thy hired servants.*

*And he arose, and came to his father, But when he was yet a great way off, his father saw him, and had compassion, and ran, and fell on his neck, and kissed him.*

*And the son said unto him, Father, I have sinned against heaven, and in thy sight, and am no more worthy to be called thy son.*

*But the father said to his servants, Bring forth the best robe, and put in on him; and put a ring on his hand, and shoes on his feet:*

*And bring hither the fatted calf, and kill it; and let us eat, and be merry:*

*For this my son was dead, and is alive again; he was lost, and is found. And they began to be merry."*

And then in Romans 8:31–39:

*What shall we then say to these things? If God be for us, who can be against us?*

*He that spared not his own Son, but delivered him up for us all, how shall he not with him also freely give us all things?*

*Who shall lay any thing to the charge of God's elect? It is God that justifieth.*

*Who is he that condemneth? It is Christ that died, yea rather, that is risen again, who is even at the right hand of God, who also maketh intercession for us.*

*Who shall separate us from the love of Christ? Shall tribulation, or distress, or persecution, or famine, or nakedness, or peril, or sword?*

*As it is written, For thy sake we are killed all the day long; we are accounted as sheep for the slaughter.*

*Nay, in all these things we are more than conquerors through him that loved us.*

*For I am persuaded, that neither death, nor life, nor angels, nor principalities, nor powers, nor things present, nor things to come,*

*Nor height, nor depth, nor any other creature,*

*shall be able to separate us from the love of*

*God, which is in Christ Jesus our Lord.*

Lastly in Romans 11:33–36:

*O the depth of the riches both of the wisdom and knowledge of God! How unsearchable are his judgments, and his ways past finding out!*

*For who hath known the mind of the Lord? Or who hath been his counsellor?*

*Or who hath first given to him, and it shall be recompensed unto him again?*

*For of him, and through him, and to him, are all things: to whom be glory for ever. Amen.*

It was that version, substantially, that Tyndale laid down his life to give us, and John Rogers and others suffered very great privation and persecution to give us. I sometimes wonder whether we, in all the luxury of freedom that is ours today, appreciate how this Book has come into our hands.

# 4.
# Modern Versions of the English Bible

We have traced the story of the English Bible from Anglo Saxon times right down to the Authorised Version (KJV) of 1611. Now, we are going to carry on from that time.

## Darby's New Translation

There were a number of versions of the English Bible that were produced between the Authorised Version (KJV) and the Revised Version during the years from 1611 to 1881. You may be interested to know, for instance, that John Wesley actually produced a New Testament in English. In fact, he was one of the first to put the New Testament into paragraphs, something which was copied later by some of the others. However, as I see it, there are two notable translations of the Bible before the actual Revised Version of 1881. The first was called *A New Translation*, and was the work of J. N. Darby. (Chronologically, it is usual to call the Revised Version the 1881 Version, even though the Old Testament was not brought out until 1885 and it was exactly the same with J. N. Darby's New

Translation of the Bible. The New Testament came out in 1871; the Old Testament came out in 1890. I have followed precedent and used the date of the first part of the work coming out in 1871.)

As most of you probably know, Darby was one of the leaders of the Brethren movement, a man greatly used of God in his day. He was no mean scholar. He was an accomplished Greek scholar and he was no small Hebrew scholar. He spoke a number of continental languages fluently. In fact, his translation of the Bible followed his translation from Greek and Hebrew into German and into French. That is no mean feat for a man whose mother tongue was English. In fact, the Elberfelder Version in German is still considered to be a very good one indeed.

His English translation, considering that it is the work of one man, is remarkably good. It is a very literal rendering and not in good English. Even though it is very stilted English, it is in fact based on very sound critical judgment. Whatever people might think about Darby and his writings, the revisers who finally produced the Revised Version of 1881 used his New Testament in their revision. It is still a very valuable translation indeed, and I might add the cheapest[1] version you can get. Because the Brethren refused to make any profit at all upon their publication of God's Word, it remains one of the cheapest and still one of the most valuable and accurate versions of God's Word, albeit not in good English.

By the way, he has the most interesting footnotes, which do require quite an amount of intelligence to understand. However, for the serious student once you have the hang of it, they are very, very helpful indeed. It was that which helped the revisers so much.

1 This was true at the time this message was shared in the 1960's

So when you consider that Darby's Version had no precedent, it had nothing to go on, it really is a remarkable feat from a man with a very busy life.

Here is one little part from J. N. Darby's Version which I think will help you to understand what I am talking about. 1 Corinthians 15:20–26: "But now Christ is raised from among [the] dead, first-fruits of those fallen asleep. For since by man [came] death, by man also resurrection of [those that are] dead." (Now, that is very bad English.) "For as in the Adam all die, thus also in the Christ all shall be made alive. But each in his own rank; [the] first-fruits, Christ; then those that are the Christ's at his coming. Then the end, when he gives up the kingdom to him [who is] God and Father; when he shall have annulled all rule and all authority and power. For he must reign until he put all enemies under his feet." That is just a little example of Darby's version.

## The Emphasised Bible

The other version that is interesting and noteworthy is a very copious volume indeed, and it is entitled the Emphasised Bible. The New Testament was published in 1872, and it was followed by the Old Testament between the years 1897 and 1902. This is again a very literal translation by a very good Greek and Hebrew scholar, J.B. Rotherham, but it sometimes makes very hard reading. It is not the kind of translation you can read just before you go to bed. It is a very helpful version but it is not so easy to read. The text is set out in such a way as to convey the most detailed shades of meaning in the original languages, hence the title, the Emphasised Bible. When you go through it, for those who cannot read Hebrew and Greek, it is very interesting to discover where the emphasis was in the original, and this Rotherham has done for us, and done very well. He has been careful about the titles of the Lord. In fact, it was the first version ever to use the name Yahweh or Jehovah for the Lord actually in the text. It is filled with treasures, but it is not easy to read at length; nevertheless, if you persevere you will find some wonderful treasures. Here are two portions that I personally have always found rather wonderful. The first is Genesis 18 from verse 9, which I think brings to life the whole story of Sarah and Abraham in a way our other versions do not.

> *"And they said unto him," (The heavenly messengers said to Abraham.) "As to Sarah thy wife ... And he said, 'Lo! [she is] in the tent.' And he said, I will, surely return, unto thee, at the quickening season—and lo! a son, for Sarah thy wife. Now Sarah, was harkening at the opening of the tent, it, being behind him. But Abraham and Sarah, were old, far gone in days,—it had ceased to be with Sarah after the manner of women. So then Sarah laughed within herself saying: 'After I am past age, hath there come to me pleasure, my lord, also being old?' And Jehovah said unto Abraham,—'Wherefore now did Sarah laugh saying. Can it really and truly be that I should bear, seeing that I have become old? Is anything too wonderful for Jehovah? At the appointed time, I will return unto thee, at the quickening season and Sarah shall have a son.' And Sarah denied, saying, 'I laughed not;' For she was afraid. And he said, 'Nay! but thou didst laugh!'"*

That brings it alive to me because Sarah was behind the flap of the tent listening. First of all, she overheard this conversation and she started to laugh within herself. Then it says, "It was the Lord, Jehovah." He suddenly turned around and spoke through the tent to her about her laughing, and she speaks through the tent to Him: "But I did not laugh." "Yes, you did." I find it very amusing to think of them holding a conversation through the actual material of the tent.

By the way have you ever realised that the emphasis is not: "Is anything too hard for the Lord?" But it is: "Is anything too wonderful for the Lord?" I have always said that. "Is anything too wonderful for the Lord?" That is rather wonderful isn't it? That is where Rotherham's version helps us to understand the shades of emphasis and meaning in the original, which the English cannot give us.

Here is another lovely little portion in Isaiah 12:2: "Lo! GOD is my salvation! I will trust and not dread,—For, my might and melody, is Jehovah, And He hath become mine by salvation."

That is beautiful, absolutely beautiful. Rotherham's version is well worth reading just to get a few nuggets like that. I wish they had brought that into the Revised Version. "The Lord is my might and melody, and he has become mine by salvation." That is beautifully put.

## The Revised Version

We come to the next really great version of the English Bible, which is the Revised Version of 1881. The Authorised Version (KJV), as I pointed out to you has been described as the greatest of all translations—the greatest of English books, the greatest of the English classics, the source of the greatest influence upon English character and English speech. If it is true on the natural level, its spiritual influence can never be overrated. Nevertheless, as time passed, it became obvious to Bible scholars that a new version was required. Indeed, as I have already said between 1611 and 1881 quite a number of new translations appeared, but none was sufficiently important to be placed alongside the Authorised Version.

## Reasons for a Revised Version

The more important reasons given for a new version are as follows. First of all, words used in the Authorised Version (KJV) had become obsolete or archaic due to the development of English over the centuries. For instance, look at Acts 19:2 in the Authorised Version: "He said unto them, Have ye received the Holy Ghost since ye believed?" This word 'since' meant something quite different in 1611. The Revised Version has quite rightly retranslated it: "Did ye receive the Holy Spirit when you believed?" That is an important point because the use of words was changing.

Again, in Galatians 1:11 is a little phrase which I think is among the more quaint sayings of the Authorised Version: "But I certify you, brethren." The word *certify*[2] has changed in its meaning today and it means something quite different. If I were to certify you, if I were qualified to do so, it could only mean one thing. But in those days it meant "I declare to you; I make clear to you."

---

2 At the time Lance shared this, the word *certify* was commonly used in the context of declaring someone insane. For example "He was certified insane," which is what he was clarifying in the above text as it had become slang.

In I Thessalonians 4:15 the Authorised Version (KJV) says, "For this we say unto you by the word of the Lord, that we which are alive and remain unto the coming of the Lord shall not prevent them which are asleep." The word 'prevent' has changed its meaning. It does not mean here that we shall not stop them, but it has been rightly retranslated, "shall in no wise precede them," "shall not go before," in other words. I suppose some of you who have studied Latin would have understood that, but many people would not. The meaning of the word has changed.

In II Thessalonians 2:7: "For the mystery of iniquity doth already work: only he who now letteth will let, until he be taken out of the way." That means something quite different and it is rightly been retranslated: "Only there is one that restraineth now, until he be taken out of the way."

In James 3:13 there is the use of the word "conversation." "… let him shew out of a good conversation his works with meekness of wisdom." This word "conversation" today means something quite different to what it meant in 1611. Then it meant, "conduct." A person's conversation was not what they *said*; it was what they lived—their conduct, their behaviour. So it had to be rightly retranslated. "Let him show by his good life his works in wisdom and meekness."

Consider even the little word in Matthew 6:34: "Take no thought for the morrow." Many people got worried about that. Did the Lord Jesus really say, "Take no thought for tomorrow"? The Revised Version has retranslated that: "Be not anxious." In fact, in 1611 "Take no thought" was a phrase which meant: "Be not anxious." It did not mean, "Do not think about tomorrow," but "do not worry about tomorrow." The Lord never told us not to think about the future, but He did tell us not to worry about the future. So you see the difference, the change in usage in English since 1611. This was one of the reasons why it was felt a new translation, a new revision was needed.

The second reason for a new translation was that in a number of instances it was felt the Authorised Version (KJV) did not represent the original. Many new manuscripts had been discovered since 1611. They were both earlier and more accurate than the ones used in the Authorised Version translation, and now these new manuscripts could be used. There was reason to believe that they represented the original more faithfully than the ones used for the 1611 version.

There was a third reason. Intensive study of the grammar and idioms of Biblical languages, along with many new discoveries of letters, correspondence, and much else to do with the days in which the Bible was written belonging to that period, had thrown much new light upon Biblical words. It was felt that now the translators could be in a position to much more accurately understand certain words in the original than they could before.

The fourth reason was a translation, however good, is always only a translation, and there is therefore great value in more than one translation. No one translation can have final authority. So these are the reasons why it was felt a new revision was needed of the English Bible.

Thus in 1870 the first moves were made, in the Convocation of Canterbury of the Church of England, which were to result in the Revised Version of 1881. It was to be a revision of the Authorised Version (KJV) in the light of new manuscripts, the new understanding of Biblical languages, and the development of the English language. The revisers were told to introduce as few alterations as possible consistent with faithfulness, while following the Authorised Version. Several scholars from various denominations were invited to join the Anglicans in this work. In fact there were some sixty-five people involved in the work—forty-one of them were Anglicans. The rest were Non-Conformists. Two companies were formed out of the sixty-five people, one for the Old Testament and one for the New Testament. Later some American scholars were invited to join in the revision and were invited to form two companies in the States. All the proofs were sent to them, and their comments and suggestions were to be made upon what they saw. There were thirty-four American scholars involved. (Now this is quite important because a little later on it has bearing on the 1901 version.)

In many ways the Revised Version differs from the Authorised Version (KJV) because of its more literal accuracy. This is the point. Its principle was a word for word translation rather than a sense for sense, or sentence for sentence translation, meaning for meaning. This has been the Authorised Version principle: sentence for sentence or meaning for meaning. Now, the revisers felt that they wanted to keep strictly to literal accuracy, and they wanted a word for word translation. It is this that has probably tended to produce rather pedantic renderings, and it is why the Revised Version has often been called the Schoolmaster's Bible.

Two of its most obvious differences are the removal, either altogether or into footnotes, of some of the passages that we all love. One of them is Acts 8:37 when Philip asked the eunuch about whether he believed with all his heart. Another is John 5:3

about the angel troubling the water, and several other passages too, which we have already dealt with in previous chapters.

The other very marked difference was the introduction for the first time of paragraphs into the Bible, done in such a way that it looked like an ordinary book. The verse numbers were inserted into the actual text, so that instead of being an obviously versified publication it was more like an ordinary book. These were the two most obvious differences in the Revised Version. It has never become as popular as the Authorised Version (KJV). Nevertheless, it remains along with its sister, the American Standard Version, the most useful and valuable version for the serious student of God's Word. I say that again. The English Revised Version, along with the American Standard Version, remains the most important, the most useful, and the most valuable of all the versions for the serious student of God's Word.

Its usefulness can be seen in a number of ways, firstly, in its literal accuracy in every way, both in the shades of meaning of words, in tenses, and in prepositions. Those of you who realise that prepositions in the Bible, especially in the New Testament do count, realise how important it is to know whether it is "in" or "with" or "through," and so on. The Revised Version tends to be literally accurate as far as possible in its rendering of prepositions and tenses and even in the shades of meaning. For instance, in the Authorised Version (KJV) in Matthew 5:29–30 and Revelation 20:13, you will find the use of the word "hell." The Revised Version correctly made a difference between these two words in the New Testament, translated by the Authorised Version as "hell." One is "hell" and means punishment by fire. The other is "Hades," and means the abode of the departed dead. In Matthew 5:29–30 the

Lord Jesus was not talking about the eternal hell of punishment; He was talking about the abode of spirits, the departed dead—Hades. However, in Revelation 20:13 you will see that the reference there is to hell itself. For it says that Hades is cast into hell. You can see straightaway that you cannot cast hell into hell; but Hades is cast into hell. So there you see it has made this distinction.

There is another little example. Take the word "sons" and "children." These two words are used absolutely interchangeably in the Authorised Version (KJV) in the most remarkable way. For instance, in John 1:12 the Authorised Version says, "To as many as received him, to them gave he power to become the sons of God." 1 John 3:1 says, "Behold, what manner of love the Father has bestowed upon us that we should be called sons of God," but the Greek original is "children of God." Most remarkably in Ephesians 1:5 in the Authorised Version we are told that we have been predestined "unto the adoption of children," and the word is "sons." Although we cannot drive too far the distinction between being sons and being children, yet there is a difference. The Revised Version, correctly, makes a distinction between children and sons, and all the way through the New Testament it keeps it clear. It calls one word "sons" and the other "children," and you don't get that in the Authorised Version. There are many other words we could mention that the Authorised Version has just used interchangeably and sometimes it seems without any real principle.

Secondly, the Revised Version is a useful version because of its literal accuracy in translating the same Greek and Hebrew words uniformly as far as is possible by the same English word. I will give you one good example of that in Mark. Whoever wrote

Mark (probably Mark) had a very interesting characteristic in his style. He used the word "straightway" so many times that it was quite remarkable. The dear Authorised Version (KJV) folk decided that they could not use the same word so many times in so short a passage. So in Mark 1:10 the Revised Version says: "And straightway coming up out of the water ..." Verse 12: "And straightway the Spirit driveth him forth into the wilderness." Verse 18: "And straightway they left their nets ..." Verse 20: "And straightway he called unto them ..." Verse 28: "And straightway everywhere the report of him went out into the whole region." Verse 30: "Now Simon's wife's mother lay sick of a fever, and straightway they tell him of her." If you look in your Authorised Version you will find "immediately," "anon," and "straightway" are used to try and break up this word occurring again and again. That is just a little example of the way the revisers felt they must translate the same word as far as possible by the same English word.

The Revised Version is very helpful because of its marginal references and its footnotes. These are most important. We cannot stay with them now, but they are in fact most important indeed for all serious students of God's Word, both the footnotes and the margin.

## The American Standard Version of 1901

The next great version of the Bible that we can talk about is the American Standard Version of 1901. Why was there an American Standard Version? How far does it differ from the Revised Version? I happen to use the American Standard Version. When the Authorised Version (KJV) was revised there were two

American companies of scholars working in the States with their English counterparts. As you would expect the Americans were neither so conservative as their English colleagues, nor were they as bound to the Anglican Church, who were the sponsors of the revision, as their English colleagues were. In the Revised Version of 1881 the American preferences are printed at the back of the English Revised Version in the appendix. You will see that all the American preferences or the American differences are printed as an appendix both to the Old Testament and to the New Testament. The American revisers were bound by an agreement not to sponsor a new edition for fourteen years after the publication of the English Revised Version, which finally came out in 1885. So the Americans were bound by that agreement until 1899. They continued during those fourteen years to study and revise further. They also had the great advantage of hearing all the criticism of the English Revised Version. Finally, due partly to the fact that in America some unauthorised pirate versions of the revision of the English Revised were being published, and partly because the American revisers naturally favoured their own preferences, variations, and renderings, they published their version in 1901.

One of its most marked departures from the Revised Version is the use of "Jehovah" instead of "LORD" in capital letters that we are used to in the Authorised Version and the Revised Version. It embodies in the text most of the American preferences for rendering. In some cases it returns to the Authorised Version and in some cases it introduces new renderings altogether. But it remains substantially the same version as the Revised Version of 1881. On the whole, the American Standard Version of 1901 generally has been considered by scholars to be the more accurate of the two versions. Many of its renderings, which differ from the English Revised Version, have been generally considered to be for the good. In fact, it is very interesting that in the New English Bible they have followed quite a lot of the renderings in the American Standard Version and in the Revised Standard Version.

I will give you a few examples where I think that the American Standard Version is superior to the English Revised Version. As you know I am not exactly pro-American, but I must say in this matter I do agree. I think most of you know that in Hebrew they used different organs of the body to explain emotions. They used bowels, kidneys, loins, heart in a way that we just do not. We only use two parts of our anatomy in this way. We speak of a person's brain or mind—he has a mind to do so and so. Or we speak of the heart. Actually, in Hebrew they used all kinds of the organs of the human body to express human emotion. Unfortunately, the Authorised Version (KJV), whether they lived nearer to the earth in those days, had no difficulty or qualms about translating bowels. As you can see in Jeremiah 4:19 it is a most awful translation: "My bowels, my bowels! I am pained at my very heart." The English Revised Version actually retranslates that. It is a most remarkable thing: "My bowels, my bowels! I am pained at my very heart." (I cannot think how the Anglicans could be quite so conservative.) The American Standard Version quite rightly translated it like this, which is beautiful: "My anguish, my anguish, I am pained at my very heart." It is obviously right. I cannot understand them rendering such a thing: "My bowels, my bowels, I am pained at the very heart."

In Psalm 7:9 we have another word. It is not quite so offensive as the previous one. "For the righteous God trieth the heart and the reins." It is a very interesting thing that the English Revised Version actually has said, "the word reins means nothing to most people; that is why we use it." That is actually what they said. They said they could not see any other way to translate this word. It meant simply nothing to most English people so they continued to use it. The English revision actually continued to use it and translated it exactly the same way as the Authorised Version (KJV). "The righteous God trieth the heart and the reins." The American Standard Version I am quite sure has rightly translated it like this: "The righteous God trieth the minds and the hearts."

In Psalm 16:7, you have the same thought again: "My reins also instruct me in the night seasons." As the American Standard revisers said, if they were to put in there "my kidneys instruct me in the night seasons" most people would be horrified. Yet that is what it literally means. Their English colleagues insisted on translating this: "My reins instruct me," which does not mean anything to anyone. So the Americans, being more go ahead, have put it like this: "Yea, my heart instructeth me in the night seasons." That makes sense. "My heart instructeth me in the night seasons." It means something.

Again, in Acts 17:22 the Authorised Version (KJV) says, "Ye men of Athens, I perceive that in all things ye are too superstitious." Do you honestly think Paul would have started off like that? The English Revised Version has put it a little bit better and said, "Ye men of Athens, in all things I perceive that you are somewhat superstitious." The American Standard Version says they were quite sure that Paul did not start off like that and what it really meant is this: "Ye men of Athens, I perceive that ye are very religious." It is very interesting that the New Revised Standard Version has done the same, and even more interesting the New English Bible has this rendering: "Ye men of Athens, I see that in everything that concerns religion you are uncommonly scrupulous." That is the idea behind it. So in many ways, the renderings of the American Standard Version, not in every case, but in many cases, are to be preferred to the English Revised Version. Unfortunately, it is now impossible to obtain it.

## Some Other Versions

There are some other versions we will swiftly mention that are not really so important. There is a little version we call the Englishman's Greek New Testament. It has the Authorised Version (KJV) in the text, the Greek text, and an interlinear translation word for word. It was brought out by Bagsters and it is in some ways quite helpful.

There is also another version, which we call the Newberry Bible. By a whole series of signs, dots, dashes, and various types, it reveals the emphasis, the tenses, etc. It was brought out in the latter part of the 19th century.

Then there was a very beautiful little version of the Epistles of St. Paul by Conybeare and Howson, which still is a very fine translation, and even more, has exceedingly helpful and exhaustive notes. It is hard to get these days. It comes from a bigger work entitled: *The Life and Epistles of Saint Paul*, and you can get it within that.

There was also another that dates from 1901: Arthur S. Way's, *Letters of Saint Paul*. This was one of the first versions to be a kind of amplified translation. In other words, he puts in a tremendous amount that is not in the original but which he believes is necessary for everyone to understand the original. In fact this little version can be quite helpful. It cannot be a serious study version, but it can be quite helpful.

There were several others. There was William Kay's Version of the Psalms and a number of other works that appeared at various points during those years.

## The Twentieth Century New Testament

However, the next great work that has appeared in the history of the English Bible is what we call the Twentieth Century New Testament. This appeared in 1902 and, in fact, was the first of the truly modern English versions. This was the parent of all the modern English versions we now have. Actually, not so many people seem to know about it. It was initiated, believe it or believe it not, by a lady called Mrs. Mary Higgs, the wife of a Congregational minister, and a telegrapher called Ernest Mallon, who was the grandson of a very well-known Swiss divine. These two got together and managed to gather together thirty men who produced this quite remarkable version. The thing that is so remarkable is not one of those thirty people who engaged on this work was either a linguistic or textual scholar or expert. In fact it has surprised many scholars since, that they did produce so fine a version. It is remarkable in that way. The concern that lay behind their producing this version was to make the Bible clear to the young people of their day in 1902.

# The Weymouth New Testament

The next version I think most of you will have heard of is of course the New Testament in Modern Speech by Dr. R. F. Weymouth. This is a lovely rendering into very dignified, contemporary English. It is a version easy to read. You can read this before you go to bed. You can read a whole letter or a whole book quite easily because it is in such beautiful, contemporary but dignified English. In fact, Weymouth was against using racy English. He said it did not become sacred themes, so he felt rather strongly about it. On the whole it is faithful to the original. It is a very valuable help indeed to anyone who wants to read straight through a whole book or a whole letter in order to get an idea of the meaning. This is a very good version. Of course, it has been superseded now by some of the more modern ones, but it is still worth reading.

For instance, here is how Weymouth puts a very involved portion in Ephesians 1:7–10: "It is in Him, and through the shedding of His blood, that we have our deliverance—the forgiveness of our offences—so abundant was God's grace, the grace which He, the possessor of all wisdom and understanding lavished upon us, when He made known to us the secret of His will. And this is in harmony with God's merciful purpose for the government of the world when the times are ripe for it—the purpose which He has cherished in His own mind of restoring the whole creation to find its one Head in Christ; yes, things in Heaven and things on earth, to find their one Head in Him." That is pretty good you know for a very, very difficult passage in the New Testament.

# The Moffatt Version

Then we come to Moffatt's Version, it is called a new translation of the Bible. The New Testament appeared in 1913 and the Old Testament in 1924. Dr. James Moffatt was a Scotsman, and he was an outstanding and brilliant scholar particularly in Hebrew and Greek. His translation of the Bible is both forceful and idiomatic more so than any that went before, and in some cases when compared to those that have come after it, as well. It has often been called The Bible in Scots because he insisted, being a Scotsman, on using Scots words. For instance, in Luke 16:1, instead of "steward" he uses the word "factor." It does not mean anything to people in the south. It has been called the Bible in Scots.

Moffatt was a confessed modernist and had no qualms at all about moving whole passages and whole chapters and certainly verses to where *he* thought they belonged. This can be a little disconcerting. He just simply chops the chapters about. As a confessed modernist, he did not believe in the inspiration, the absolute authority of God's Word. He believed it contained it, and he had no qualms at all about moving bits and pieces around. It is very disconcerting in certain parts. He certainly realised his avowed aim to make the original speak in English in its own forceful way. No version is as forceful as Moffat's. Everyone agrees, right down to the modern translators, that he had a tremendous gift for putting the Hebrew particularly into just the English that it needed.

In Nahum 3:1–3, which is not an easy book to read:

*O city soaked with blood! Crammed with lies and
plunder—no end to your ravaging! Hark, the swish of the
whip, hark, the thunder of wheels, horses a gallop, chariots
hurtling along, cavalry charging—the flash of the sword,
the gleam of the lance, the slain in heaps, dead bodies
piled, no end to the corpses—men tripping over the dead!*

That is the original, and it has been lost in many of the versions.
Everyone agrees that this is the finest version of Nahum.
Nahum 3:11–19:

*So you too will stagger and swoon, you too will fly for refuge
from the foe; all your forts are but fig trees—your defenders
the ripe figs—shake them, they drop into the hungry mouth!
The men inside you are but women! Your bars are burned
by fire, the gates to your land fly open in front of your foe.*

*Draw water for your siege, strengthen your defences:
down with you to the mud, trample the clay. All hands
to the brick-mould! But there will the fire devour you,
the sword will cut you down. Multiply men like locusts,
multiply men like grasshoppers, let your traders be more
than the stars of heaven!—yet locusts spread their wings,
and your half-breeds are like locusts, your officers like
grasshoppers, huddling in hedges when the day is cold, and
flying when the sun is up, flying none knows where.*

*Assyria, your rulers are asleep, your lords slumber in*
*death! Your people are scattered all over the hills, with*
*none to rally them. You are shattered past repair, wounded*
*to death. All who are told of you clap their hands over*
*you; for whom have you not wronged unceasingly?"*

Now that is forceful and idiomatic, and there is no version that has translated the Hebrew quite as Moffatt has. Sometimes I am afraid his forcefulness resulted in very unfortunate renderings indeed, and it is nowhere more apparent than in the Song of Solomon. In chapter 1, verse 3, the Authorised Version (KJV) has here: "Therefore do the virgins love thee." At the end of verse 4 the American Standard Version puts it like this: "... rightly do they love thee." Moffatt horrified the Christians of his day by translating this: "The girls are all in love with you." Verse 4: "... no wonder the girls adore you." He insisted that was the original, and he would not have anything said against it.

In Song of Songs 2:13 the Authorised Version (KJV) says very beautifully, "Arise, my love, my fair one, and come away." He rendered it to the horror of many people: "... come, dear, come away, my beauty!" Of course, we know this is a love story, but it absolutely shocked the people of his day. Nothing had ever appeared like it before and to most Christians it was horrifying.

Again, in chapter 7:1 the Authorised Version (KJV) puts this lovely little word, and I remember Hudson Taylor has such a lovely note on this: "How beautiful are thy feet with shoes." (It does sound a bit funny.) Moffatt puts it: "How neatly you trip it, O princess mine."

Again, in chapter 8:8–9 where the Authorised Version (KJV) has such a stately rendering, Moffatt renders this in a way that again went against him in the eyes of most Christian people, the lay people: "We have a young sister, and she has no breasts yet; but what shall we do with our sister, when her wooers come? If she holds out like a wall, we will adorn her with silver for dowry. If she gives way to lovers like a door, then we will plank her up." It is just quite amazing. Moffatt, I am afraid was not exactly received with wide open arms by many Christian people.

Moffatt also allowed his own strong convictions to influence his treatment of the text. I have already pointed out his removal of various parts of God's Word to where he thought they belonged. I will give you an example of this which is absolutely amazing. In 1 Timothy 5:23 there is a verse Paul wrote to Timothy in his first letter: "Take no more water but take a little wine for your stomach's sake." Dr. Moffatt was a well-known total abstainer. He was violently against alcohol, and his conviction was so strong that he was convinced that the apostle Paul never ever gave such advice. So he took it out of the Bible altogether and put it in a footnote. This is what he said and it is not even in the text. In his little footnote he says, "The words, 'Give up being a total abstainer; take a little wine for the sake of your stomach and your frequent attack of illnesses,' are either a marginal gloss or misplaced." He had absolutely no authority whatsoever for saying it, and no one has ever supported him. They may have talked about other things but never, never that.

Yet, the amazing thing is that for all the faults of Moffatt, his version is remarkable. Sometimes it is the most helpful version of all if you want to understand some of the books of the

Old Testament. If you want to read right through a book, Moffatt is sometimes the one that is the most helpful. Sometimes in places he rises to supreme heights. I do not think his version of 1 Corinthians 13 has ever been bettered. He puts it like this:

*I may speak with the tongues of men and of angels, but*
*if I have no love, I am a noisy gong or a clanging cymbal;*
*I may prophesy, fathom all mysteries and secret lore, I*
*may have such absolute faith that I can move hills from*
*their place, but if I have no love, I count for nothing. I may*
*distribute all I possess in charity, I may give up my body*
*to be burnt, but if I have no love, I make nothing of it.*

*Love is very patient, very kind. Love knows no jealousy;*
*love makes no parade, gives itself no airs, is never rude,*
*never selfish, never irritated, never resentful; love is never*
*glad when others go wrong, love is gladdened by goodness,*
*always slow to expose, always eager to believe the best,*
*always hopeful, always patient. Love never disappears.*

That is really terrific!

## The Knox Version

The next version we can consider is Monsieur Knox's version. We will not say a lot about it. The New Testament came out in 1945, the Old Testament in 1949. This is a translation of the Latin Vulgate in the light of the Greek and Hebrew original. It is therefore a translation of a translation. It is rendered in the most beautiful English and makes very good reading. It is, of course, a Roman

Catholic version, and it reflects Roman Catholic teaching in its footnotes. In parts, Knox is superb. For instance, F.F. Bruce says he does not think Chronicles is rendered anywhere better than by Knox. After reading Moffatt's version of the Song of Solomon, Knox's version of the Song of Solomon is simply wonderful. It has been considered to be the best English version. That is saying something, isn't it, for a Catholic? It is a good additional version to have if you want now and again to read it.

## The Revised Standard Version

Then we come to the Revised Standard Version which many of you use. The New Testament came out in 1946, the Old Testament in 1952. This is a revision of the American Standard Version of 1901 in the light of all the latest discoveries and understanding. It was made by thirty-two American scholars—not by British but American scholars wholly. It has swung away from the more literal renderings of the Revised Version and the American Standard Version back to the principles of the Authorised Version (KJV) of 1611. Rather than word for word, it is a freer translation— sense for sense. In some ways it swung too far in that direction, covering some of the finer distinctions especially in the New Testament. This is one of the criticisms against it. Nevertheless, it is a very good version. It is in good English and it is free from Americanisms. It has a few American spellings, but that is all. It is also, and I believe this is important, free from unfortunate peculiarities, which is saying something when you remember these studies we have had on God's Word. It went back to LORD of the Authorised Version and Revised Version instead of the Jehovah of the American Standard Version. Now I must say and underline this, that this version is invaluable to the serious student of God's Word. You should have a Revised Version or an American Standard Version, and the Revised Standard Version. These two are an absolute must for the serious student of God's Word.

## The Phillips Version

Then we come to the Phillips Version and this is a very interesting version indeed. It came out fully completed in 1958. In fact, the work had begun much earlier. It first came out as *Letters to the Young Churches*, and then all the other portions were finished bit by bit until finally in 1958 it was brought out completed.

Of all the modern versions, Phillips seems to have found the most universal and real acceptance by Christian people. Indeed, it has become the most popular version since the Authorised Version (KJV). Did you know that? It has had higher sales than any of the versions of the Bible other than the Authorised Version. This is quite remarkable. It is a direct translation from the original and is in the most racy and colloquial English. No other version speaks the language of the man in the street in quite the same way as Phillips. Phillips himself said that he felt when he translated the Greek that it was like rewiring a very ancient house without being able to turn off the main. In many ways his version has got just that atmosphere about it. You really do get shocks in it just because it is so up to date and so racy. In many ways one prefers it to the New English Bible, although, of course, it is much more racy and colloquial and even uses slang in some cases.

Here are some examples of that. In Luke 15 from verse 14, you have a wonderful version for the man in the street: "And when he had run through all his money, a terrible famine arose in that country, and he began to feel the pinch. Then he went and hired himself out to one of the citizens of that country who sent him out into the fields to feed the pigs. He got to the point of longing to stuff himself with the food the pigs were eating, and not a soul gave him anything."

It is interesting that the New English Bible has taken over "he began to feel the pinch," but it stopped at the "stuff," I am glad to say. That is slang, not just ordinary English. "He stuffed himself" really is slang. It is hard to believe that the Lord used language like that, and yet it may well be.

Again, in John 7:46: "No man ever spoke as this man speaks!" they replied. "Has he pulled the wool over your eyes, too?" retorted the Pharisees. "Have any of the authorities or any of the Pharisees believed in him? But this crowd, who know nothing about the Law, is damned anyway!" Now that is getting very near to slang.

Again, in Romans 6:1, which is a doctrinal passage: "Now what is our response to be? Shall we sin to our heart's content and see how far we can exploit the grace of God? What a ghastly thought!" Really, you should not use language like that. That is slang. Every time he used the word "God forbid," he used this phrase: "What a ghastly thought!" Nevertheless, it must be said that it was Phillips' aim to produce the same effect on twentieth century readers as the original did on 1st century readers. On the whole his rendering is vital and gripping.

For instance, look at 1 Corinthians 2:2–4. I think this is terrific. I can imagine Paul writing like this. "You may as well know now that it was my secret determination to concentrate entirely on Jesus Christ himself and the fact of his death upon the cross.

As a matter of fact, in myself I was feeling far from strong; I was nervous and rather shaky. What I said and preached had none of the attractiveness of the clever mind, but it was a demonstration of the power of the Spirit!" I am quite sure that is how Paul wrote.

There is another little portion in II Corinthians 11:17–21. It is an outburst of Paul and I am sure this is how he wrote the letter because it is not really in such good Greek. "I am not now speaking as the Lord commands me" (What a thing to write!) "but as a fool who must be in on this business of boasting. Since all the others are so proud of themselves, let me do a little boasting as well. From your heights of superior wisdom I am sure you can smile tolerantly on a fool. Oh, you're tolerant all right! You don't mind, do you, if a man takes away your liberty, spends your money, takes advantage of you, puts on airs or even smacks your face? I am almost ashamed to say that I never did brave strong things like that to you. Yet in whatever particular they enjoy such confidence I (speaking as a fool, remember) have just as much confidence." Now that is terrific really, and in our versions you do not get that.

In Philemon, verses 10–18, we have this:

*No, I am appealing to that love of yours, a simple personal appeal from Paul the old man, in prison for Jesus Christ's sake. I am appealing for my child. Yes, I have become a father though I have been under lock and key, and the child's name is—Onesimus! Oh, I know you have found him pretty useless in the past but he is going to be useful now, to both of us. I am sending him back to you. Will you*

*receive him as my son, part of me? I should have dearly*
*loved to have kept him with me: he could have done what*
*you would have done—looked after me here in prison for*
*the gospel's sake. But I would do nothing without consulting*
*you first, for if you have a favour to give me, let it be*
*spontaneous and not forced from you by circumstances!*

*It occurs to me that there has been a purpose in your losing*
*him. You lost him, a slave for a time; now you are having*
*him back for good, not merely as a slave, but as a brother*
*Christian. He is already especially loved by me—how much*
*more will you be able to love him, both as a man and as a*
*fellow Christian! You and I have so much in common, haven't*
*we? Then do welcome him as you would welcome me. If you*
*feel he has wronged or cheated you put it down to my account.*

That is beautiful. This version I believe is particularly helpful
in involved doctrinal passages. The charge is often made
against it that it is not a translation; it is a paraphrase. Of course,
there is a lot of truth in the charge, although strangely enough,
Professor Bruce defends this version to the hilt. He says that,
in fact, where the translation ends and the paraphrase begins is
very, very hard to define. In fact, he says this is a meaning for
meaning translation. Certainly it is one that many of you could
afford to have, for it is the easiest of all the versions today to read
and certainly challenges you all the time.

# The Amplified Bible

There is also the Amplified Bible. I am not going to say very much about it because I want to get through the other versions. The New Testament of the Amplified Bible came out in 1958, and the Old Testament in 1962. This is a new translation with alternative meanings or additional words to bring out the sense of the original incorporated in the text. In other words, it is another expanded translation. One must, of course, be very, very careful with expanded and amplified translations. Nevertheless, it is undoubtedly very helpful and valuable to many people. I will give you one little instance of this.

In John 1:12 it says, "But to as many as did receive and welcome Him, He gave the authority, (power, privilege, right) to become the children of God, that is, to those who believe in (adhere to, trust in, and rely on) His name."

Then, here is a little example from the Old Testament in Psalm 84:4: "Blessed (happy, fortunate, and to be envied) are those who dwell in Your house and Your presence; they will be singing Your praises all the day long. Selah [pause, and calmly think of that]!" That, I am afraid, is most unfortunate. However, they evidently felt that is what it means.

# Thompson's Chain Reference and the Scofield Reference Bible

There are also two other study versions which I would like to mention just in passing. There is a huge volume called Thompson's Chain Reference Bible, and (I do not have a copy; I am not sorry), the Scofield Reference Bible. These two are study versions of the Bible, and in some ways you have to be very wary of them, especially with the Scofield. He was a brilliant man and a sound man, but he introduced into the text a whole system of theology and doctrine, even to chronology and dispensational teaching, which is incorporated within the text. The uninitiated may tend to think this is as inspired as the Word itself, and because of this it can become very dangerous indeed. If you do use those versions, use them with care and they can be helpful, especially Thompson's Chain Reference. Scofield's can be to a certain extent, but I personally am very much against those that incorporate all these things too much into the actual text itself.

## The Barclay Version

There is another version before we come almost to the end, and it is the Barclay Version. I do not suppose very many of you have heard of it. It was brought out fully in 1958. Professor Bruce describes this as a conservative counterpart to the Revised Standard Version. (I expect you all know there was great controversy over the Revised Standard Version when it came out.) This is the counterblast of more conservative theologians. It is not a revision but a new translation from the original by twenty America conservative scholars. I am not talking about their political colour; I am talking about whether they are fundamentalists or modernists. They were fundamentalists, theologically conservative scholars—all known believers. They felt there was need for a version to be brought out by men who knew the Lord, and they thought that a new version should be brought out for the use of those who did not want to touch something which they felt to be polluted. That might be a little unfair to put it like that, but certainly it was some part of the motive that was behind it. Its footnotes are clearly those of evangelicals. Great care has been taken in this version over messianic prophecy in particular. The great charge against the Revised Standard Version was that in several instances it toned down what was clearly messianic prophecy. (I am not going to go into whether or not that is true.) However, the Barclay Version was very careful to make sure that it was put back again.

In the Revised Standard Version in Isaiah 7:14, you have this: "Behold, a young woman shall conceive and bear a son and shall call his name Immanuel." That caused a terrible uproar amongst fundamentalists in the United States of the more rabid type because they felt that the virgin birth of the Lord Jesus had been done away with.

In this Barclay version they put it like this: "Therefore, the Lord Himself will give you a Son; behold the virgin shall conceive and shall bear a Son and call His name Immanuel." There are many other ways in which they bring out messianic prophecy, rightly or wrongly. It is very accurate in its translation, but much could be said about its style. I am afraid that even if they were born again believers the style is sadly lacking. Indeed it is! In some cases I cannot believe some of the things that have got into it. I am not trying to be funny but you ought to know some of the things that have been put into this version. These are the things that ridicule God's people. In Psalm 42:11, it says: "Why are you bowed down oh my soul? why do you groan within me? Hope in God for I shall yet praise Him my face-saver and my God." "My face-saver" It is true, but it is awful!

Isaiah 43:5: "Hope in God; for I shall yet praise Him; my face-saver and my God." In chapter 44:12 one tends to blink a bit at this kind of rendering. "Thou didst sell thy people dirt cheap."

In Romans 9:27 you tend to have a little bit of a shock when you read this. "Even though the number of Israel's sons were as the sand of the sea, the leftovers shall be saved," instead of the "remnant." Of course, it is literal, "the leftovers shall be saved." It is amazing.

Then there is this amazing little bit in 1 Corinthians 11:1, which is not even English: "Pattern after me as I pattern after Christ." Can anyone make that out?—"pattern after me as I pattern after Christ." It is not even English.

I think, without wanting to be nasty or vulgar that the most amazing thing of all is that fearful one in Jeremiah 4:19. I quoted this one a little earlier, and I do not know how it ever got through the editorial committee of this version: "My pain, my inside, let me rise; walls of my heart, my heart is torn within me." One feels like giving him a dose of Enos (a digestive aide). "My pain, my inside ..." I do not know how people could render God's Word quite like that. It is rather remarkable to say the least. However, it will no doubt be revised, and perhaps some of these more amazing bits will be toned down.

## The New English Bible

Finally, we come to the New English Bible. The New Testament was published in 1961, and is now the latest and final one so far[3]. From Tyndale's New Testament in 1525 right the way down to the Revised Standard Version of 1946, including the ones after it, nearly all these versions can be traced back to one source and tradition. This new and latest version that we call the New

---

3 At the time this ministry was given in the early 1960s, it was the latest version to have been printed. The New English Bible Old Testament was brought out in 1970.

English Bible is not a revision but an altogether new translation apart from all previous versions. It remains to be seen how successful it will be. It began in 1946 with a proposal in the General Assembly of the Church of Scotland, which resulted in approaches being made to both the Anglican and Free Churches, and the appointment in 1947 of a committee representing all the major denominations to be in charge of this translation. Its aim was to produce an altogether new translation of the Bible in what they called timeless English. In other words, it was not to be in slang, it was not to be in English too modern that it will quickly date, but to be put into what they called timeless, contemporary English. Their aim was not to replace the Authorised Version (KJV), but to produce a new translation to be placed alongside the Authorised Version or Revised Version. It has gone back to the older principle of the Authorised Version in translating sense and meaning rather than a more literal rendering of word for word. Its English is good, but one is bothered about the way it translates certain phrases. I will just give you an example of this that bothers me personally. I do not know how much it bothers others, but this is the kind of thing I find bothering.

John 3:14–15: "This Son of man must be lifted up as the serpent was lifted up by Moses in the wilderness so that everyone who has faith in Him may in Him possess eternal life." This bothers me: "has faith in Him." They have consistently rendered it: "has faith in Him." I cannot understand why they did not use the much simpler English word *trust* because in many ways it is very difficult to translate the word used. I think even Phillips is superior to this rendering when he translates it *believes*. He just goes back to the old word and translates it believes.

Another little example is John 1:12: "To all who did receive Him, to those who have yielded Him their allegiance." Now that is a translation of "those who believed on His name." It is lovely, "yielded Him their allegiance," however I am bothered about it because I am not sure that you can translate even those that believe on His name in that way. In other words, if it ever came to the time when people took this as their study version they would not even know the name of the Lord was in that verse. Therefore all the preciousness of the name would be lost to them. Now, that is what makes me realise that this version in its present form of English will be useful to us for reading and certainly useful in parts when we are reaching the unsaved. However, I doubt very much whether it will ever to able to become a serious study version. So far there is nothing that can take the place of the English Revised Version or the American Standard Version or even J. N. Darby's version along with the Revised Standard Version and some of the modern versions. Personally, I think if you have the English Revised, the Revised Standard Version and Phillips you have three very good versions indeed by which to seriously study God's Word.

In many ways it is an interesting study we have taken, but we must finish. Perhaps the best way we can finish is by reading a passage we have read several times, which I think is rather fine in this version (New English Bible).

1 Corinthians 12:31b—14:1a:

*And now I will show you the best way of all. I may speak in tongues of men or of angels but if I am without love I am a sounding gong or a clanging cymbal. I may have the gift of*

*prophecy and know every hidden truth, I may have faith
strong enough to remove mountains, but if I have no love
I am nothing. I may dole out all I possess or even give my
body to be burnt, but if I have no love, I am none the better.*

*Love is patient, love is kind and envies no one. Love is never
boastful nor conceited, nor rude, never selfish, nor quick to take
offense. Love keeps no score of wrongs, does not gloat over other
men's sins, but delights in the truth. There is nothing love cannot
face; there is no limit to its faith, its hope, and its endurance.*

*Love will never come to an end. Are there prophets? their
work will be over. Are there tongues of ecstasy? they will
cease. Is there knowledge? it will vanish away; for our
knowledge and our prophecy alike are partial, and the
partial vanishes when wholeness comes. When I was a child,
my speech, my outlook, and my thoughts were all childish.
When I grew up, I had finished with childish things. Now
we see only puzzling reflections in a mirror, but then we
shall see face to face. My knowledge now is partial, then it
will be whole, like God's knowledge of me. In a word, there
are three things that last forever: faith, and hope, and
love, but the greatest of them all is love. Put love first.*

That is a fine rendering.

# 5.
# How to Study the Bible

We have now looked at many aspects of the Bible. We have looked at the matter of authority, of inspiration, and of revelation. We have looked at the aim and the scope of the Bible[1], its structure and its growth, the text and its transmission over the centuries, and we have dealt with the history of the English versions of the Bible. Now it remains for us to consider the way we should approach personal Bible reading and the study of God's Word.

There has been an awful lot in these studies that has, of necessity, been technical. However, we must point out that in every way God's Word can meet us. There is, in fact, no part of God's Word which God cannot use at some time or other to really meet us in our need. It is interesting, for instance, to discover that in Matthew 13:19 and onwards, God calls his Word "a seed." It is a seed which is sown in us, and it will convert us. It will grow and bear fruit—much fruit, in fact.

---

1 See Part 1 of *How the Bible Came to Be*

In 1 Peter 2:2 we are told it is "milk." When we are very young and we cannot take solid food, then God's Word is milk to us. So you must never think that once God has sown His Word into your heart, it has taken root, it is beginning to grow, and you are a true child of God that now there is not something in God's Word for you. However simple your outlook, however young you are as a Christian, there is something for you. God's Word is called milk, and we are told to desire it as newborn babes.

Then we are told in Hebrews 5:14 that when we are a little older there is solid food. When we have got beyond the milk stage, we still need milk, but there is solid food in the Bible for those who are full-grown.

Then again, in Psalm 119:105 we are told that God's Word is a lamp to lighten our path to guide us. Do we need guidance? Do we need to know something of the situation we are in? Do we need to understand God's will for our lives? Do we need to understand God's purpose in its most general and greatest lines? Well, God's Word is a lamp. Not only will it give us personal light and show us the way, not only will it lead us, as it were, into all truth, but it will show us a much greater scale if we would know what is the purpose of God from eternity to eternity.

In James 1:23 we read that the Bible is a mirror in which we can see ourselves. There is very great need for us to see ourselves, to see whether we are growing in the Lord, to see what is ugly, to see what is untidy, to see what needs cleaning up, to see just what we are like. God's Word is a mirror and if we are honest as we come to God's Word, we see things as they really are. We shall see a reflection of things in God's Word that will tell us the truth about ourselves, and it is no good saying that reflection is someone else. That reflection is me. I am looking into it. So, God's Word is a mirror.

In Jeremiah 23:29, God's Word is called a fire that burns and purifies. It burns up the dross and purifies what is true and valuable. God's Word is like that if you and I are honest. If we want to go on with the Lord, then God's Word will be a fire in our bones. If we allow the Lord to have His way, it will burn up what is dross and it will purify what is of Himself. "The words of the Lord are pure words; as silver tried in a furnace on the earth" (Psalm 12:6). It is tried by fire.

Then again in the same verse (Jeremiah 23:29), we are told that God's Word is a hammer and it breaks what has got to be broken. If there is something in you that has got to be broken, you can be quite sure that God's Word will break it in the end. God's Word is a hammer. Sometimes we do not like certain parts of God's Word. There are some people who only read certain portions of God's Word because they know those are the comforting portions. I always feel a little fearful about "promise boxes" in that direction, for you cannot fail to get some comforting promise from a promise box. But God's Word is a hammer at times, and it is for our own well-being that part of our nature gets broken. If there is something in us that needs breaking then thank God, God's Word will break it. It is a hammer in the hands of the Holy Spirit.

In Ephesians 5:26 we are told that God's Word is a laver, a washing bowl, a washing place. There we can be washed continually and we can be kept clean. Jesus said, "You are clean through the word that I have spoken unto you." The Psalmist said, "Thy word have I hid in my heart, that I might not sin against Thee" (Psalm 119:11). God's Word is a laver and every time we read God's

Word it cleanses our mind. Are you troubled by evil thoughts? Read God's Word. You will find it has a cleansing effect upon your mind. Are you bothered about other things? Do you feel dirty? Read God's Word. You will find it cleanses you. Somehow it purifies the atmosphere; it purifies the mind. "You are clean through the word which I have spoken unto you." God's Word is a laver and the priest had to continually come back to the laver to wash in it. Therefore, you and I have got to continually come back to God's Word that we may be washed; we may receive that washing by the Word.

Then, in Ephesians 6:17 God's Word is a sword. In Hebrews 4:12 it is a sword that does something in us. It is a sword that divides soul from spirit. It is really almost like a surgeon's knife. God's Word can be like that. It is not a blunt instrument, not an instrument that hacks its way into you. It is just like a surgeon's knife, and God knows exactly what He is doing. By His Word He can sever things; He can get in on the inside and say, "That is Christ, and that is you." He can discern the thoughts and intents of the heart by His Word. "Search me, oh God, and try me, and see whether there be any wicked way in me" (see Psalm 139:23–24). God's Word is also a sword to be held in our hand for defence and for victory. In Ephesians 6:17 we are told that it is the sword of the Spirit which is the Word of God. Get it into your hand and you will be able to withstand the devil in the day when he comes. When the evil one comes, you will have God's Word in you and you can deal with the evil. You can defend yourself by the Word of God, and not only defend yourself, you can overcome the evil one by the Word of God.

God's Word is all these things. We have been talking about a lot of the technicalities of God's Word—the structure of the Bible, the growth of the Bible, the text of the Bible, but this is the thing that is the most important. This is the way God uses His Word with us and to us. In the light of all that, I want us to consider how we should personally read and study the Bible.

## Read God's Word Above All Else

The first thing I would like to underline is the need to be careful not to substitute books *on* or about the Bible for the Bible itself. It is an amazing fact that all of us have a tendency to more easily read books on the Bible than the Bible. For instance, I know some people who take Scripture Union notes and other notes, and in some cases they read the notes and do not read the Bible. It is an amazing fact! We must be very, very careful not to substitute books on or about the Bible for the Bible itself. One can read a commentary, for instance, and really virtually only read the commentary and not the Bible's text. You can read a helpful book, an exposition shall we say, on some chapter of the Bible, but in fact you are not reading God's Word itself. It may be a helpful and valuable commentary and exposition, but it is not God's Word itself. It is a comment upon God's Word. Now, this is very important because it is a danger we can all easily fall into—reading and studying books in place of the Bible.

I suppose it hardly needs to be said that such books have got their place. They are legitimate and they are valuable. But if reading them is substituted for reading the Bible itself, then they become positively dangerous. A good and legitimate thing has become a means of keeping you away from the original contact with God's Word. You are reading God's Word in a second-hand way. Instead of getting right through to God's Word itself and letting the Holy Spirit use it in your heart and life, you are taking something that has had meaning to someone else. Exposition, commentaries, Bible notes, and much else have a place. I am just pointing out that it can be positively dangerous if we read those things in place of the Bible.

## Read God's Word Itself

The thing to remember and do is to read and study God's Word itself above all else. It is a strange thing that we often find almost an aversion within ourselves to reading God's Word. We have a natural, should I say, traitor within us. Often there is an aversion within us, which we may not even recognize, to reading God's Word. We can spend hours reading the newspapers or a novel. We can spend hours reading books, but when it comes to reading God's Word there is a strange aversion to it. We have difficulty over it. We just do not want to or we say we find it "hard going." Isn't it strange that we do not find this about other things, but only when it comes to God's Word? I think that we have got to take very real note of this because Bible study can become not only vital, valuable, and instructive for us, but it can become enthralling. I do not know why people should think Bible study is always tedious, why they feel that it is some terrible duty through which they have got to plod. Do you know Bible study can become absolutely enthralling? I am not saying that it will always be exciting or enthralling. There are times that we have got to plod. There are a whole lot of reasons for that. We sometimes get out on the wrong side of the bed in the morning, and whatever we do somehow or other is wrong. However, what I am saying is that Bible study need not only be valuable, instructive, and necessary, but it can be enthralling if it is approached in the right way, and that is the point of this study.

Of course, if every single morning you are given awful, lumpy porridge that does not have enough salt in it, followed by a terribly hard-boiled egg and tea that looks like dishwater, I do not wonder that you long for a continental breakfast of one little roll and a nice cup of coffee. Of course, you do not relish your breakfast, and you do not look forward to it. A little bit of variety, a little bit of better cooking, a little bit more care and your breakfast will be something that you will look forward to. It is not only necessary, not only important, but there will also be something you look forward to. That is exactly the same with Bible study, and I am not being irreverent. If a little more time is taken over it, a little more care given to it, a little more preparation, a little more variety in the way that you approach it, your Bible study, your Bible reading will not only be vital, but it will also become enthralling.

## Be Determined to Make Time

Firstly, therefore, there are two things to remember: we must read God's Word itself. Now get that into your head. I know it is terribly simple, but we must read God's Word itself. That is the first thing. The second thing is that a determination is needed to ignore feelings and make time. I have found that this aversion that is often inside of you, once it is ignored and you make time, you are enthralled. Often, those are the times the Lord meets you most especially. It is just as if in the unseen the evil one knew there was a blessing for you that morning, so he has tried to put you off.

Determination is needed. Do not just think that is the old man. Some people seem to think that any determination belongs to the old man, that it is the flesh life. No! There can be a determination of the right kind. We must fight the good fight of faith and lay hold on the life eternal (1 Timothy 6:12). Determination is needed to ignore these feelings and to say you are not going to have anything to do with them. You have got to feed.

Suppose day after day you refused to eat because you did not feel like it. Well, in the end you would starve to death. You have got to pull yourself together and eat! Likewise, you have got to eat spiritually. The devil knows this only too well, and he will inject some kind of drug into you spiritually that will just take away your appetite. The pills called purple hearts,[2] do you know what they do? They take away your appetite, and you could go without eating for a year. That is what the devil does with some people. He gives them a spiritual "purple heart" and after a while they lose their appetite for God's Word. They seem all right, but gradually, they begin to collapse. We can all see it; the backbone is going, there is a dullness in the eye, and a pallor in the face. They are going down slowly because they have lost their appetite for God's Word. All they have to do is pull themselves together and say, "It is necessary for me to have a daily meal spiritually." That means determination to ignore my feelings and to make time! Someone said, "You will never have time for reading God's Word or for prayer until you make it." It is very true. If you wait for some little opportunity during the day, you will discover that a whole week

---

2 Purple hearts were amphetamines that were commonly used in the 60's as a dietary aid. They also came to be abused and used like speed.

has gone by and you have had no opportunity. The opportunity and the time have to be made.

## Take Bible Study Seriously

Another important thing is that there is a need to take Bible reading and study seriously! It is no good taking it in a light-hearted frivolous way. Why don't you get more out of your Bible reading? You are not taking it seriously, that is why. You fall out of bed, put a comb through your hair, sort of look rather bleary eyed at the mirror and you start to brush and clean yourself up. Then you have your breakfast, and three minutes between then and catching the bus, you race through the *Daily Light*, not even the Word of God. (Mr. Redpath once called it "the lazy man's Bible.") So you race through it and you are off. Then you say, "I do not know why, but I have lost my appetite for spiritual things." Of course you have lost your appetite for spiritual things. You will never get anywhere until you take Bible study seriously. Do you really think that God is going to take you seriously if you do not take Him seriously? Do you really think the Lord Jesus who said, "Do not cast pearls before swine" (Matthew 7:6) is going to open up the treasures of His Word to you when you are just crawling around the place, devoting just a rushed minute in which you are thinking all the time about getting away, and your mind is on other things? No, no, not at all!

### Search or Investigate

There are four things in God's Word that show us how we must seriously treat the reading and study of His Word. First, in Acts 17:11: "Now these were more noble than those in Thessalonica, in that they received the word with all readiness of mind, examining the scriptures daily, whether these things were so." The Authorised Version (KJV) has "searching the scriptures daily." In fact, the word means "investigate." These people examined or investigated the scriptures daily. If you are going to take Bible study seriously, the first word to remember is examine, search or investigate.

I looked the word up in Vines dictionary and I found a very interesting thing. This word means "to examine by torture." It was used, for instance, when Pilate spoke of the Lord Jesus, "I have examined Him, and find no fault in Him" (see Luke 23:14). The word is to examine very carefully under torture. It was used in that connection anyway. You see, this is the kind of word that God uses. Bible study is not to be confined to a rushed few moments. You have got to *examine* carefully; you have got to *investigate* the Word of God. That is very important. It is to be thoroughly investigated and searched out. It is like a mine of precious things. In a mine men have got to go right down into the darkness and work hard to get those precious things out. God's Word is like a mine; it yields to hard work, real examination, and investigation.

## Meditate

The second word is in Joshua 1:8: "This book of the law shall not depart out of thy mouth, but thou shalt meditate thereon day and night, that thou mayest observe to do according to all that is written."

Psalm 1:2: "But his delight is in the law of the Lord; and on his law doth he meditate day and night." There you have it—meditate. We need to give time to reflection. It is very interesting that the

Hebrew word means, "mutter." The idea is that of someone who is so lost in meditation that they are muttering to themselves. They are turning it over in their heart and they are lost in thought. That is the word—lost in thought.

Now, do you take the study and reading of God's Word so seriously that you meditate on it? We find in these days that meditation is a lost art. Do you reflect upon what you read? Do you meditate? God's Word is food, and it must be digested. Therefore, you must not only read God's Word, you must think upon it. You must reflect upon it. You must be lost in thought upon it.

## Compare

In 1 Corinthians 2:13b it says, "… comparing spiritual things with spiritual" (Revised Version). It is not a very easy sentence to translate, and you will find the versions differ, with all of them having marginal alternatives. But the word that I want to remind you of here is compare. We need to *compare* scripture with scripture all the time, remembering that the Bible is an unfolding revelation.

Second Peter 1:20 says, "Knowing this first, that no prophecy of scripture is of private interpretation." In other words, no scripture can be uniquely interpreted; it cannot be interpreted on its own. Every scripture must be seen in the perspective of the rest of scripture. In other words, learn how to compare scripture with scripture.

Second Timothy 2:15 says, "Give diligence to present thyself approved unto God, a workman that needeth not to be ashamed, rightly dividing the word of truth." Originally, the word was "rightly dividing, cutting, or dividing." Then it came to mean, "dealing rightly." We must learn how to deal rightly with God's Word. Only the Lord knows how terribly His Word is sometimes treated, how people tear it out of context or how they wrongly divide it. They do not compare scripture with scripture. If you are going to take Bible reading seriously compare scripture with scripture. Learn to rightly divide and handle aright the Word of God.

## Obey

Lastly, in taking Bible reading and study seriously, obey God's Word. James 1:22a, "But be ye doers of the word, and not hearers only." John 7:17: "Anyone who resolves to do the will of God will know whether the teaching is from God or whether I am speaking on my own" (RSV). Do not expect God's Word to be opened up to you if you are not prepared to obey; it is a closed book. Many people come to me and say, "The Bible does not speak to me as it should." Yes, the Bible will not speak to you if you are not prepared to obey. If any man's will is to do the will of God, he shall know of the teaching that it is from God. If your will has not capitulated to the Lord Jesus Christ and if you are not prepared to obey Him, then do not expect God's Word to open up to you. Taking God's Word seriously means that you are not looking upon it as something to be trifled with, something just to be played around with, a little bit of intellectual study or a little bit of adding to the brain, as it were. No, God's Word will not open up to that at all. We must learn to obey.

# Prayerfully Rely on the Holy Spirit

The third thing in studying and reading the Bible is the need of prayerful reliance upon the Holy Spirit continually. The Bible is mere literature to the natural mind. It is a great mass of religious law, of story, of some history and doctrine to the natural man. Its real meaning is hidden to such. It is true to say the Bible is a closed book to the natural man.

First Corinthians 2:12–13a and 14–15 say, "But we received, not the spirit of the world, but the spirit which is from God; that we might know the things that were freely given to us of God. Which things also we speak ... Now the natural man receiveth not the things of the Spirit of God: for they are foolishness unto him; and he cannot know them, because they are spiritually judged. But he that is spiritual judgeth all things, and he himself is judged of no man."

Second Corinthians 3:14–16: "But their minds were hardened: for until this very day at the reading of the old covenant the same veil remaineth, it not being revealed to them that it is done away in Christ. But unto this day, whensoever Moses is read, a veil lieth upon their heart. But whensoever it shall turn to the Lord, the veil is taken away."

There is a veil over the heart of the natural man. You can even be a converted person and still have a veil over your heart. The Bible is a closed book, an absolutely closed book, unless you really have been brought into an experience of the Spirit of God. It is the Spirit of God that really begins to lead us into all truth.

This is exactly what the Lord Jesus spoke of in John 16:13a and 14, "Howbeit when he, the Spirit of truth, is come, he shall guide you into all the truth ... He shall glorify me: for he shall take of mine, and shall declare it unto you."

In John 14:26 the Lord Jesus said again, "But the Comforter, even the Holy Spirit, whom the Father will send in my name, he shall teach you all things."

In Ephesians 1:16–18 Paul gets on his knees and he prays for the church at Ephesus. He prays that there may be granted unto them a spirit of wisdom and revelation, the eyes of their hearts being enlightened that they might *know*. Do you wonder why Paul did not write to the church at Ephesus and say, "Now here is my letter, and I believe it is absolutely from God, so all of you get down to studying it. That is all you have got to do"? He did not say that. He wrote that he was getting on his knees and praying that the eyes of their heart may be enlightened that they might know what he was talking about.

In other words, you can have the letter to the Ephesians, you can have this whole book and study it, get hold of its doctrine and teaching and yet remain spiritually in the dark. It is because the spirit of wisdom and revelation in the knowledge of Christ has not been granted to you; the eyes of your heart have not been enlightened that you might know. You cannot just approach the Bible as you do Shakespeare, or the Koran, or something else like the great Chinese classics. You have got to approach this Book in prayerful reliance upon the Holy Spirit. Do you know I never read this Book without praying first that the Holy Spirit would lead me? I was taught to do that when I was first saved, and I have done it all the way through my life that I can remember.

I remember that dear old lady, Aunt Edna, who had quite an influence on me when I was younger. She used to say many times to me, "Do not ever open that Book without asking the Holy Spirit to lead you!" That got into my heart and I cannot read this Book without asking the Holy Spirit to reveal it. I always ask the Spirit, "Holy Spirit, Lord, You know I am blind! I am absolutely blind to this Book! Please lead me into the truth" and it has been my experience that the Holy Spirit has led me into the truth. The little that I know I owe completely to the guidance of the Holy Spirit. Why did John the apostle say, "You have an anointing from the Holy One, and you know all things ... you need not that any one teach you; but as his anointing teacheth you concerning all things"? (1 John 2:20, 27b). It does not mean that you do not need teachers. There are functions and gifts in the church of teaching, but you have within you the Holy Spirit who can reveal these things originally. You not only hear it from the platform, but it is being made real to you inwardly so that it becomes original and you do not have second-hand experience.

Whenever there is no real revelation or enlightenment of the heart by the Holy Spirit, all experience and all knowledge is second-hand. When fascism or communism or whatever antichrist force finally comes, that kind of second-hand Christianity will be the first to go. It will shift overnight. It will be gone in a flash. People will not be prepared to lose everything for Christ's sake. No, the whole point is to have an original, inward knowledge of the Lord. How does that come? By you and I getting on our knees prayerfully.

Really, there is a strange arrogance, a strange pride in us all that stops us from doing this. It is as if we are giving something away when we get down on our knees. Of course, we are because when we get down on our knees, we are just saying, "Lord, in these matters I am a simple fool and I need the Holy Spirit." That is the kind of attitude the Holy Spirit really takes up. Once you say, "I am a simple fool in the things of God," the Holy Spirit will say, "Well, I will start to educate you." But if you think that you have got a brain, a mind, an intellect, and all the rest of it you will get yourself into such a mess. You will have it all up there in your head and you will be barren down in your heart, and you will blame it on everyone else. You will go around saying, "Ohhh! They are this ...! They are that ...! They are the other ...!" When, in fact, it is *you*! You! It is all in your head and not in your heart! You cannot blame them or anyone else. Provision has been made for every one of us by Christ that we might have an original experience of the Lord.

Never study the Word of God without first praying for the Holy Spirit's gracious ministry of guidance, enlightenment, and instruction. If you ever read Scripture Union notes you ought to know that because at the beginning of every portion there is a little prayer for the guidance of the Holy Spirit. I fear many people overlook that, but it is the best thing about Scripture Bible Notes.

## Approach the Bible Humbly

The fourth thing in the way we study God's Word is the need of humility in our approach to the Bible. God does not *have* to open up His Word to us, and if there is any trace of arrogance, He will not. There has got to be humility. This is really what it means when a person gets on their knees like a little child and asks the Lord by His Holy Spirit to lead them into all truth. We must have humility when we approach God. We must recognise that this is God's Word! It's like it is hidden. The vast part of God's Word is hidden from the wise, but revealed to babes and sucklings. We need to be very, very humble when we come to God's Word.

When we come up against a problem or a difficulty that we do not understand in reading God's Word, pray and ask the Lord, "Lord, will You show me what this means?" If the Lord does not show you what this means, be humble enough to let it go and leave it; concentrate on what you do understand. You can be absolutely sure that in the little portion you are reading there is something for you. Concentrate on what God is saying and let go of what you do not understand.

I learned this lesson in Egypt. I had a dreadful kind of mind which was like a dog worrying a bone or a cat watching a mouse. It was the kind of thing that I could not let go. I used to get hold of a problem, say for example, in the book of Acts: "All those that were foreordained unto eternal life were saved." I would get hold of that, and I would worry and worry myself about it, thinking, "Then how can it say 'whosoever will, may come?' How can it say that?"

I remember once when I was in Port Said I ruined one of the times of two dear old missionaries when we were gathered around the table in the morning with an open Bible. I was worrying and worrying and worrying about this problem, and I could not get an answer from them. So I said, "But there must be some answer!" Finally, the older one of the two said to me, "You must be humble in your approach to God's Word. I have studied the Bible most of my life," she said. She showed me her Bible, which had very wide margins and there were written notes in her handwriting. Against some were a question mark and a date. Then underneath was another date and it just had: "Understood."

She said, "Now you see, when I came up against that problem I could not understand, I said, 'Lord, are You going to show me this today?' Then I would think about it and nothing would happen. I did not worry about it, for I had learned the lesson to be humble in the approach to God's Word. I put a question mark in the margin and put the date. Sometimes it so happened that I heard a word and I thought, 'That is it! Explained.'"

"Or," she said, "I went back to it and was reading again, and I saw a question mark. I thought, 'What was wrong with me then? That is perfectly plain to me. Why ever did I put a question mark in there?'" So then she would put next to it "understood" and put the date.

There, you see? That is what happens if you grow, if you are humble enough to leave things and grow. Of course it does not mean that we should put up with all kinds of problems and mysteries in the Word. However, when you come up with a problem in your reading or study of God's Word, ask Him about it. If He does not reveal it to you, go on like a child. Do not bother about what you cannot understand; go on to what you can. Do you know if you bother (like I used to) so much about what you cannot understand you will not get that which you can? You are so bothered about circling round and round that it is like a whirlpool. You are sucked into it and you never get to the harbour. So remember, humility is very important.

## The Helpfulness of Bible Aids

The fifth thing I want to say is about the helpfulness of Bible aids. I have said some harsh things about commentaries and notes and so on, and I am not going to take those back at the present. However, I am going to say that Bible aids (and they are different from Bible commentaries, notes, exposition and so on) are invaluable.

What are Bible aids? If you want to study and read God's Word seriously, you must have a good concordance or a good word dictionary, such as *Young's Concordance*. Every single word in the English Bible is in this volume. All you have to do in the Authorised Version (KJV) rendering is to find the word and look it up. There you will find all the different words translated by that one word and you will find out the shade of meaning of the particular word that is in the verse or passage you are reading. It is invaluable! Once you have started using a concordance it is well worth the money to get a concordance like that because it is invaluable to Bible study. I am not talking about that little *Cruden's Concordance* that is so in fashion amongst many of you; I am talking about *Young's* or *Strong's*. *Cruden's* only tells you a particular word and where it is used, but it does not tell you if it is the same Greek or Hebrew word or a different one. But *Young's* will tell you immediately exactly what word is used and what particular shade of meaning it has. I could say an awful lot about that, but there we are.

There are two good New Testament Bible dictionaries. One, the simplest person should be able to use, is *Vine's Dictionary of New Testament Words*. Really, you do not need much intelligence to use that. Then there is *A Critical Lexicon and Concordance* by Bullinger. That is another marvellous work. Thus, if any of you want to really understand the meaning of a word you must have one or the other of these dictionaries. These are Bible aids. They do not tell you what the compiler thinks, they tell you what it *means*. That is all. That is what you and I want to know, isn't it? We want to get down to what God's Word means, and these are Bible aids to our understanding of God's Word.

For example, in John 21 Jesus said, "Lovest thou Me?" (It has a little number in the Revised Version or the American Standard Version.) Peter answered, "Lord, thou knowest that I love Thee." But you would not know by just reading it that there are two different words used. The Lord Jesus used one word for love and Peter replied with another word for love. Then the Lord used His word again, "Lovest thou me, Peter?" and Peter used his word again. Then the Lord used Peter's word the last time and Peter used it back: "Thou knowest that I love Thee, Lord." You would not know that just by reading your ordinary English version, but you will find it in the concordance or in a good word dictionary.

The second very helpful thing in Bible aids is a good Bible dictionary, not a word dictionary, but a Bible dictionary. One is *Fausset's Bible Encyclopedia and Dictionary* and the other is the new IVF (InterVarsity Fellowship[3]) one. Personally, I think this Bible dictionary of the IVF is really undoubtedly the best. However, Fausset was a dear, old godly man and although this volume is now a little dated, it is still a mine of spiritual wealth.

Why do we need a Bible dictionary? Take for instance the word "seals." What do you know about the word seals? Does it mean anything to you? When we look it up in the Bible dictionary, we find everything about seals in the Old Testament and in the New Testament. There are illustrations, you are told something about the history of ancient seals, and it is all explained to you. We discover, for instance, something very, very wonderful in the

3 This dictionary is now published by InterVarsity Press

New Testament use of the term "seal." The ideas of ownership, authentication, and security predominate. Then it goes on to tell you where and how. For example, in one case, "Sealed with the Holy Spirit" really means the marriage bond. Do you see? You would not really know that unless you had a Bible dictionary.

There is another word you might look up—"watchman" or "watchtower." Do you know anything about that? If you look it up in your Bible dictionary you will get a lot of help because you will find that watchtowers were used for two different purposes in Biblical times. Firstly, towers were built from the earliest times in the past to protect cattle and sheep against animals and thieves. It is possible that towers were erected in vineyards and cornfields for protection against thieves. Secondly, towers of a more complex structure were built in the defence works of larger cities. In the watchtowers the watchmen were on the alert for hostile action against the city. They were also there to give word to the king of any person approaching the city wall. In time of hostility the dangers of the night were especially feared, and the watchmen eagerly looked forward to the break of day.

Thus you begin to understand what it means when Habakkuk says, "I will get me out into my watchtower." He is talking about the break of day! He is going to get up there and watch and guard. He has got the things of God, His interest, you see? He is there to defend it spiritually and wait for the break of day. Well, I do not know whether that helps you, but it helps me.

Then there is another Bible aid, a good English dictionary. This helps us in understanding words. Many people do not really understand the words we even commonly use. Sometimes it is necessary to have an *Oxford Dictionary* for when we are thinking, "Oh, what does that word mean?"

I once knew a person who thought that "undertake" only meant taking away dead bodies. So they got a bit surprised about the hymn "He Will Undertake," although I am sure they got some spiritual benefit out of it when thinking of the cross. Nevertheless, it is amazing what people do think. We are all such proud people that we will not tell each other what we really think a word means. I always used to pronounce the word *misled* as *misselled*. I could never understand the word. I used to think, "I wonder what that word *misselled* means." We never used to like to ask anyone. In fact, it was *misled*. However, you need a good English dictionary to discover what these words mean.

Another useful Bible aid is found in the Bible itself in good versions of the Bible. It is the marginal references. These references are in the columns of the American Standard Version certainly, and of the Revised Version (not the footnotes of the Revised Version). The best cross-references are found in the Revised Version and the American Standard Version. A lot of thought and care went into their compilation. They are in fact invaluable.

Let me give you an example of this very swiftly in Exodus 13:21: (of course you are probably using various versions) "And the Lord went before them by day in a pillar of cloud." In my version where it says, "And the Lord ...," just before "the Lord" there is the little letter $x$. If I look in the margin I see $x$ and I read "chapter 14:19." Now I read, "And the angel of God, who went before the camp of Israel, removed and went behind them; and the pillar of cloud removed from before them, and stood behind them." Then it says in verse 24: "And it came to pass in the morning watch, that Jehovah looked forth upon the host of the Egyptians through the pillar of fire and of cloud, and discomfited the host of the Egyptians." This gives cross-references to other references of "the pillar of cloud and fire."

Chapter 33:9–10 I read again, "And it came to pass, when Moses entered into the Tent, the pillar of cloud descended, and stood at the door of the Tent: and Jehovah spake with Moses. And all the people saw the pillar of cloud ..." Psalm 78:14: "In the day-time also he led them with a cloud, and all the night with a light of fire." Psalm 99:7: "He spake unto them in the pillar of cloud ..." And then lastly Psalm 105:39: "He spread a cloud for a covering, and fire to give light in the night."

Do you see? You have had a whole little Bible study on the pillar of cloud and fire in different connections and all are following cross-references. Do you ever look up cross-references? The best way to get to know your Bible and to understand the meaning of things is to use the cross-references. They are there for you. Not only that but use the other marginal notes or footnotes that give alternative or variant readings. These are all useful Bible aids.

## Devotional Bible Reading

I would like to go on to say something about devotional reading of the Bible. We can never overemphasise the need to regard God's Word as our spiritual food. Therefore, we need to take some part of it each day and thoroughly digest it. We can never overemphasise the need of taking some part of God's Word and digesting it each day. If you have one huge meal and you do not eat for a week, you will suffer physically. I will not tell you how, but you will suffer because you are meant to have regular meals, not to gorge now and again. It does not do you any good. Consequently, spiritually you need to feed regularly upon God's Word. It is good to have a definite scheme or plan of reading, rather than to be haphazard. There are some people I know who love to be haphazard. They just open their Bible in the evening and read the first bit that their eye lights upon. If the Lord blesses them, I am very glad. However, I think that it is much better to have a definite scheme or plan for reading God's Word.

There are many schemes. My Bible has a scheme by which you can read the whole of the Bible in three years from end to end. Perhaps that is a bit too ambitious for some of you, so why not take a book and read a paragraph a day. Do not overdo it. Do not try to read a whole chapter a day. Just read a few verses every day. I take it you have already prayed the Lord would lead you, guide you, and instruct you by His Holy Spirit. Give time for reflection and meditation over these few verses you are reading. Look up the marginal cross-references, follow them and you will begin to get very interested. Some of them are dead ends and you will think, "I do not know why they have a cross-reference to that." But there are others that will help you and you will be thrilled! You will think, "That throws light upon it." Find out the meaning of the words which are important in that particular verse or passage. If you have got to look them up in the concordance or the dictionary, look them up. If there is some custom or some event or something that you cannot understand from just reading the Word, look them up in the Bible dictionary.

For this kind of Bible study you need the Revised Version, the American Standard Version, or even J.N. Darby's version. These three versions are absolutely excellent for this kind of reading. They are important versions. Also, the Amplified can be very helpful for this kind of devotional reading. You cannot read great chunks of the Amplified because it is hard reading, but you can read a few verses like this. You can think about it and it can be really helpful if you read it comparing it with the Revised Version or the Authorised Version. Indeed, if it is a short passage you read each day, you can even compare it in various versions such as Weymouth, Phillips, or the New English Bible. Have them by, open them up, and just compare; you will be thrilled; you will be enthralled. Gradually, you will feel you are getting somewhere, you are understanding something. That is the way to read God's Word devotionally.

## Comprehensive Bible Study

Then, I would just like to say something very briefly about comprehensively studying the Bible. I have used this word comprehensive study of the Bible with the idea that there is a very real place for reading a whole book through, and it is an essential form of Bible study. This is something you will have to do at another time, but this is when you can have a gorge. You are having your regular meals, and every now and again you are going out for a good Chinese meal or up to town for a very big meal.

You can take a book and read through from beginning to end without any reference to chapters and verses at all. Ignore them altogether as if they did not exist and start from the beginning and read right the way through. You may think: "He must think we have got an awful lot of time." Now listen, in this kind of study you do not need such a lot of time. You can read through some of the letters in literally a quarter of an hour. It is the chapters and verses that slow you down. When you forget those you can read through Philemon in four minutes. Jude you can get through in three minutes, right through beginning to end. Even the book of Job, which has a large number of chapters, you can read in two hours from beginning to end. Of course, you cannot read the Psalms right through, but they are not meant to be read right through like that. However, these other books you can read right through from the beginning.

Did you know that Campbell Morgan never preached from a book of the Bible until he had read it through consecutively fourteen times? Did you know that brother Nee read through the New Testament twenty-one times from the beginning of Matthew to the end of Revelation before he first started to preach? He sat down and read it through again and again. Do you know how long it will take you to read the whole Bible through from beginning to end? Sixty-six hours, so it is reckoned.

The whole point is that there are some books of God's Word that you can certainly read right through, and it is very, very important to do so. I must say this however, and this is probably what gives you the problem. It is hard to read a book through in the Authorised Version (KJV), or even the Revised Version. For the New Testament you want to read it in Phillips, or Weymouth, or the New English Bible. All these are helpful in reading through from beginning to end, and it will not make you tired. If you read Phillips right through you will not be tired; you will be quite excited, much more so than the newspaper. It really is tremendous once you really get into it!

For the Old Testament, although Moffatt does change the verses around a bit, if you can get over that business, he is marvellous for reading through a whole book of the Old Testament. Even Professor Bruce says he's invaluable. There are some books of the Old Testament you cannot read through in any other version from beginning to end. Knox's version is another one you can read through a whole book in the Old Testament from beginning to end. And of course there is the Revised Standard Version. Read through a book in these different versions and gradually you will grasp the overall theme, but you will have to do it again and again. However, if you mean to study God's Word seriously, that is the way to do it. Start at the beginning and read right through, and you will begin to understand it. After a while it will dawn on you and you will be thrilled at what does dawn on you.

In this type of Bible study it is sometimes good to understand a little of the authorship, the date, and the background. In the versions that are designed to be read like this, you will often find in Phillips and the others, he has in fact given you the data you need at the beginning for this kind of Bible study.

## Analytical Bible Study

There is another kind of study of the Bible we can call the analytical study. I am not going to say a lot about this because it is so common. This is an absolutely exhaustive way of studying God's Word and one of the most valuable. How do you do it? It is not so much concerned with the book and the overall theme as the meaning of each phrase, almost each word. So it is a verse by verse, phrase by phrase study of the Bible using the cross-references, using the concordance, and using other versions.

The first time I really got an appetite for studying God's Word was in Egypt. It was in that little missionary home in Port Said where two sisters, (of course they were retired) would clear everything away after breakfast. One sat at one end of the table and the other one would sit at the other end of the table with their big Bibles open. All the other versions were on the table along with the big concordance. When I first went there, I just gasped! I had never seen people study the Word like that. This was a real meal. We used to spend an hour on one verse; we never moved off it! They would go through it and one would say to the other, "Now, what do you think this means?" Then the other would say, "Well, do you know what I think *this* means? So and so and such and such ..." They would look somewhere in Ephesians and then they would look in Revelation. They would look it up in the concordance, and then they would see what it says in Conybeare, and then look somewhere else. It was absolutely thrilling to hear what came out of those studies with those two old ladies! They were tremendous! I have been to some big conventions, and have not received as much out of those meetings as I have out of the times with those two old ladies. They were walking Bibles. I used to say I had never met any couple like it.

When I was younger I had moved quite a bit amongst people who were quite high up in evangelical circles, but they did not know their Bibles. However, those sisters really knew what it was to study the Word, and they had studied it exhaustively. I also saw that they got so much enjoyment out of it and it was not heavy. It was so light and so living that I was absolutely enthralled. Do you know, that gave me my first real appetite for God's Word. Ever since then I have studied it like that. It gave me an appetite!

Of course, there is nothing like seeing someone else enjoying God's Word because you start to get an appetite don't you? You think, "Well, if they are enjoying it there must be something in it!" That is analytical study of the Word.

## Topical Bible Study

There are three other ways of studying the Bible that we can look at. There is the topical way of studying God's Word. What do I mean by topical way? Well, take types or symbols as your study. For instance, take the dove. Take your concordance and look up the word *dove*. Then look up every single reference in the Bible to the word *dove* and think about it. It is a wonderful Bible study. If you were to do it you might be really thrilled! You go right from the beginning and you begin to find Biblical typology. Oh, it is thrilling!

Take the vine. Look up the word vine in your concordance, and then go right through the Bible, looking up every reference to vine, and you will be thrilled! That is the way to do it! If you have gotten a bit tired of the other way, go to the topical way and there are lots of other subjects I could give you.

Then there are places to study. Think of the word *Hebron*. Do you know what the word *Hebron* means? It means company or fjord. It is the place in the river where people have to cross together, so it came to mean fellowship. Now take the concordance, look up the word *Hebron* and look up every single passage. You will get an illumination on historical events you never had before. Fellowship is the key and you will think, "My word, David was crowned at Hebron!" It is fellowship!

There is *Jordan* which is another symbol. When you find this word *Jordan*, every time it speaks of the cross, death to self. Oh, that is wonderful!

There are events that you can study. Take *exodus* and look up every reference to the exodus in the Bible. That should keep you going for a month, and you will have a real Bible study there.

Then there is the occurrence of certain words. Have you ever thought of the word *worship*? Look it up in the concordance and find the first time the word *worship* is ever used. Then look through every occurrence of the word *worship*. It will take you a long time. You can do it day by day, but you ought to be a worshiping Christian by the end of it!

Then there is the word *glory*. Look in your concordance for the first time the word *glory* is mentioned, and go right the way through to the last chapter in the Bible till you have got the last occurrence of the word glory. It will give you an understanding of things you have never had before. That is the topical way of studying God's Word.

## Biographical Bible Study

Then there is the biographical way of studying God's Word. Take Demas as an example. Look up Demas in the concordance and you will find he is mentioned three times. In Philemon Paul says, "My beloved fellow worker, Demas." The second time he mentions him chronologically is in Colossians and it is "Demas," no "beloved fellow worker." The last time he is mentioned is in II Timothy, "Demas hath forsaken me, having loved this present world." You have got a biography. Three verses! Now then, those of you who have got a train to catch in the morning, there are three verses. That is enough to think about the whole day. Some of you might need it too!

Then, of course, you think of David. Have you ever thought of studying David in relation to his Psalms? Well, I will tell you how to do it. Find a book about David's life, and there are two I will mention: one is by Alexander Whyte, a wonderful one on the life of David as found through his Psalms. Another wonderful one is F.B. Meyer's *David*. Begin to read it as a Bible study. I know I said earlier, don't read books on the Bible, but here is one that you can read because it is biographical. As you begin to read the Psalms you can set them into the life of David! It will thrill you! You will begin to understand the Psalms in a way you never understood them before. Why did he say what he said? How did he praise the Lord when he was in that scrape?

## Studying Prophecy in the Bible

Lastly, another way of Bible study is prophecy. Of course, you have got to be careful here because you can go off the rails; yet we must give the due and rightful place to prophecy. In Scripture there is Messianic prophecy, which is prophecy to do with Christ, and there is other prophecy. Begin to study it. Trace the whole story of prophecy right through from the beginning. Study fulfilled prophecy. It is wonderful to study fulfilled prophecy. Then, when you finish studying fulfilled prophecy, begin studying unfulfilled prophecy. Because just as surely as God has fulfilled a certain amount of prophecy, He is going to fulfil the rest.

These are all ways of studying the Bible. There is no need for Bible study to be heavy and hard and difficult. You have got to give time, you have got to be serious, and you have got to rely upon the Holy Spirit, but Bible study can be enthralling! Of course, that is not its main objective, to enthral us. The objective of the Holy Spirit is that we might be fed by God's Word, we may be corrected by God's Word, we may be built up by God's Word, we may be strengthened by God's Word, we may be brought unto full growth by God's Word, and we may be able to minister to others through God's Word. We are to be fed, and instructed, and enlightened through the Word of God. Nevertheless, it does not have to be a penance. I am sure the Lord never gave us this wonderful, wonderful Book that Christians might suffer over it, sort of with an ice bag on their head and a cup of strong coffee by their side, burning the midnight hour, saying, "Oh, what a penance Bible study is! How difficult and laborious it is!" God gave us His Word that it might really help us in order that we might every time go away and say, "Oh, how unsearchable are the ways of God, past finding out!" That is how we should go away from an atmosphere like that every time, "Oh, is this the Word of God? How amazing! How wonderful! How gracious of God to bring a sinner like me into an understanding like this!"

Shall we pray?

*Our dear Lord Jesus, we do pray that the result of this time might be that we all really do study and read Thy Word. Oh, make us a people who really do know something of the inward meaning of Thy dear Word. It cost Thee so much, Lord, to give it to us. It has cost others so much to bring it to us in English. Lord, we pray that we might forever appreciate the cost and the sacrifice behind it and may treat it with the reverence it deserves. We ask it in Thy name. Amen.*

# 6.
# Taking the Bible Seriously

We are now going to turn back to the second point that we made previously in our study on how to read and study the Bible. It is the need to take Bible reading and study seriously. We pointed out that unless we really do approach this whole matter of the way we read and study the Bible seriously, we cannot possibly expect to get much out of it. If we simply skim through a few verses or read a passage so that at the end of it we do not even know what we have read—our minds, in fact, have been thinking about something else while our eyes have been reading the words—we should not expect to get anything out of God's Word. The more seriously we approach the reading and the study of the Bible, the more we shall receive from it. We have said a lot about the way we should approach it and many other matters, but now I would like to spend a little more time on the four points that we mentioned in taking Bible reading and study seriously. We spoke of searching, meditating, comparing, and obeying. So we will just look for a little longer at this whole matter.

# The Powerful Word of God

One thing we can say about God's Word is that it has within it the power to do something in us. This, I am afraid, is often not realised. This Book is different from all other books in the sense that when the Holy Spirit takes the words of this Book and makes them live, He is able to effect in us what we read in the Book. This is what we call revelation, but it suddenly comes in a flash. You could have studied something, you know all about it, and then all of a sudden it is revealed to you. In an instant, that which is revealed to you becomes somehow your experience.

For instance, in II Corinthians 4:6 Paul says, "Seeing it is God, that said, Light shall shine out of darkness, who shined in our hearts, to give the light of the knowledge of the glory of God in the face of Jesus Christ." The interesting thing is that Paul compares this word with the way that God spoke in the beginning when He said, "Let there be light." And in Genesis 1 you find: "and it was so." In other words, as soon as God said something it was done. So it is with us, God's Word has the most tremendous power to do something; it is, in fact, creative.

In II Peter 3:5, 7a we have the same idea: "For this they willfully forget, that there were heavens from of old, and an earth compacted out of water and amidst water, by the word of God … but the heavens that now are, and the earth, by the same word have been stored up for fire." The fact is that God's Word is creative. When God says something, it is done. He does not just say a few words and they remain theory. When God says something, what He says has the power within it to do His will, to actually effect His will, to influence, to change and mould things.

If you and I came to God's Word in that light, if we looked upon it as the greatest moulding force in our lives, it would transform our reading and the way we approach God's Word. The whole matter comes down to the fact that God can use this Book to do something in us, and if it is approached in the right way He will do just that.

## Examine

The first thing we mentioned about taking Bible reading and study seriously was the word *search* or *investigate*. Acts 17:11 says, "Now these were more noble than those in Thessalonica, in that they received the word with all readiness of mind, examining the scriptures daily, whether these things were so." The Authorised Version says, "… searching the scriptures daily as to whether these things were so." This word is, in fact, very interesting indeed. There are three ways that we can look at this word; all basically meaning the same thing, but each way of looking at it just brings some fresh aspect of taking Bible reading and study seriously.

Firstly, it means to 'examine,' and this is the favourite word of the modern versions. It is used when Pilate said of the Lord Jesus, "I have examined Him" (see Luke 23:14). It was the technical word used for examination by torture. In the old days when they examined a person, when they interrogated them, they did not just ask them some nice questions across the table and leave it at that. They brainwashed them on the rack, or by being whipped, or torturing them in other ways. In this way they were examined under torture.

This is the word that is used here of the Scriptures. "These people were more noble than those in Thessalonica …" because they examined the Scriptures exhaustively. The idea is of a careful, analytical examination as by a magnifying glass or under a microscope. It is an examination of God's Word minutely.

Are you taking your reading of God's Word seriously like that? Are you examining it minutely? Are you taking the very words that are used and thinking about them? Are you asking yourselves, "What does this word mean?" Are you looking up the cross-references? Are you examining each part of God's Word? This is why the folk at Thessalonica were commended. They not only heard what was said on the platform, they not only heard what the apostle and others said, but they went back home and put what was said under the microscope of God's Word and looked very carefully: "Now, is this thing so?"

Oh, if only there were more of that amongst us! Not just taking what the speaker says, whoever he is, but taking what he says as coming from God, going home and examining it as to whether it can bear examination. Really, carefully, analytically, examining all and everything in the light of God's Word, for that would bring us into very great blessing.

Some people hear, "This is the purpose of God, and so and so and so and so." Then they say, "Of course, Lance said that is the purpose of God, so it *must* be the purpose of God." Or they say, "Mr. Sparks says that this is the purpose of God, so it *must* be the purpose of God." Or brother Nee says, "This is the meaning of the cross, so it *must* be the meaning of the cross." Or Billy Graham says, "This is the meaning of the church, therefore it *must* be the meaning of the church." Do you see what I mean? We ought to take what these dear brethren say and examine it in the light of God's Word. Don't just pretend or copy the Word of God or just swallow it whole, but microscopically examine what God's Word says concerning this. If that was the way that we approached the reading and the study of the Bible, oh what the Lord might be able to do none of us have yet conceived!

God's Word is the most dynamic power in the universe. It is not just the written Word. Once it is approached in the right way, once you rely on the Holy Spirit, God's Word is like the atom. Once it is split, once it is opened, what power is inherent within it! It can change things! It can affect things! It can influence things in your life. If only you and I would allow God's Word to do something in us!

But if we want God's Word to do something in us, we have got to allow it to do something in us. We have got to get to God's Word, not to things *about* God's Word. We have got to get to the pure source, the fountainhead and get to God's Word itself. We have got to take God's Word itself and examine it carefully. Now I wonder whether you and I are examining God's Word.

I will give you a few examples from my own experience. For instance, Psalm 37:1–5 says, "Fret not thyself because of evil-doers, neither be thou envious against them that work unrighteousness. For they shall soon be cut down like the grass, and wither as the green herb. Trust in the Lord, and do good; dwell in the land, and feed on his faithfulness. Delight thyself also in the Lord; and he will give thee the desires of thy heart. Commit thy way unto the Lord" (asv).

Now then, don't just read it very quickly like the speed of a train going through. That is no good at all! You may have to cut back to one verse each time. For example, take just verse 5: "Commit thy way unto the Lord." What does it mean to commit thy way unto the Lord? It is no good merely repeating it over and over, but what does it mean? Ask yourself, what does this word "commit thy way unto the Lord" mean?

Now, the first thing is that it is to the Lord! It is not to a thing, not to a movement, not to the saints, not to truth, but to a Person. Commit thy way unto the Lord. That is tremendous!

What does *commit* mean? You must sit down and think. Put it under a microscope. My version has a little *k* there, and when you look it up it references Psalm 55:22: "Cast thy burden upon Jehovah, and he will sustain thee" (ASV). This is the cross-reference. "Commit thy way unto the Lord" and "cast thy burden upon the Lord and He will sustain thee." Now, does this throw light upon it?

There is a footnote in my version, and it has a little *8* by "cast thy burden." The footnote says, "What He has given me." Well, isn't that beautiful? I am getting a blessing already. "Commit thy way unto the Lord," I have found out that the little cross-reference is "cast thy burden upon the Lord." Burden–"Oh, I am so burdened." Perhaps some of the burdens I have got are my own fault. I am so glad it says, "Cast thy burden upon the Lord." But look at *this*: "Cast what he hath given me upon the Lord." Isn't that beautiful! It's what He has given us. "Commit thy way unto the Lord; cast thy burden upon the Lord; cast what He hath given thee upon the Lord." Well, what has He given you? He has given you a job to do, and it is a big burden. Cast what He has given you upon the Lord. That is rather wonderful.

Then I go back to my first reference again, *k*, and I see it refers to Proverbs 16:3: "Commit thy works unto the Lord and thy purposes shall be established." So we have "commit thy *way* unto the Lord," "cast thy *burden* upon the Lord," cast *what He hath given thee* upon the Lord," and now "commit thy works unto the Lord." What are your works? Commit thy *works* unto the Lord and He will care for thee. Isn't that wonderful?

If I go back to Psalm 37 and look at the cross-reference again, I see *k* and it says 1 Peter 5:7. So now I turn to the New Testament: "Casting all your anxiety upon him, because he careth for you."

This is the microscopic examination of God's Word. We have taken only five minutes to go through all that from "commit thy way unto the Lord." Look where it has got us! Isn't that enough food for you for the whole day or perhaps for the whole week? You can live on that! When it is your works that are troubling you: commit thy works unto the Lord and He will establish them. If you have a burden: cast thy burden upon the Lord. If you are full of care: casting all your care upon Him for He careth for you. Or if you are not really sure about your way, commit your way unto the Lord.

But just wait. Let's return again to Psalm 37:5. We must ask ourselves what it means to commit. If you have a footnote, it says, "Hebrew: 'Roll thy way upon the Lord.'" This gives us an alternative shade of meaning: "roll thy way upon the Lord." It is not only commit thy way unto the Lord, commit it over into His care, make Him manager of it, make Him Lord of it, commit it over to Him, but now it is "roll it" upon the Lord. It has become a big boulder, a great burden. Get behind it and get it moving and roll it. Once you have got it rolling it will not stop, and just keep it rolling until you have got the whole thing well and truly upon the Lord. "Roll thy way upon the Lord and trust also in Him, and He will bring it to pass." That is a microscopic examination of God's Word.

## The Right Approach to God's Word

Some of us are dead spiritually, not only from the neck upwards, but also from the neck downwards because we do not allow God's Word to do its work. Then we come and say, "Well, I do not know what it is. It is all second-hand and it does not mean a thing to me. I find myself utterly bored." The whole point is that Christianity is nothing unless it is original. It is like everything else—you can just take it on. The only way you can stop yourself from taking these things on is by reading God's Word yourself. It is no good reading God's Word in a sort of thick-headed, 'wooden' way. It will not do anything for you at all. You might as well read Shakespeare.

The whole point is that if you want God's Word to do anything for you, you have got to approach it trusting the Lord. You have got to use your intelligence, but your intelligence must first be broken of its own self-sufficiency so that it rests on the Holy Spirit. Then you can use your intelligence as much as you want. The Holy Spirit will see to that. The more you do, the more God will speak with you and  the more He will do for you.

I read something that I thought was very true. It was said by Martin Anstey. (He is in the presence of the Lord now.) He said that if the Bible does not separate you from your sin, your sin will separate you from the Bible. Think about it. Generally speaking, if we are not really reading God's Word, we can be sure there is sin somewhere.

## Investigate

The second idea of this word *search* is *investigate*, not only to examine microscopically, but also investigate. The idea here is one of thoughtful consideration, not only examine microscopically, analyse, but investigate it. Go right through the thing and try to find out as much as we possibly can; really investigate it. Of course, it is the same idea as examination, but it just has this slight difference.

I thought of one or two instances. One is in Isaiah 53:4: "We did esteem him stricken, smitten of God, and afflicted" (ASV). Supposing, as I suggested before, you are engaging in an analytical study of God's Word, that is word by word, and you are looking at this and thinking about, "Surely He hath borne our griefs and carried our sorrows; yet we did esteem him stricken, smitten of God, and afflicted." If you look at the Revised Standard Version, it says more or less the same. If you look at Moffatt it says something in a little more modern language. Then you look at Knox's Latin Vulgate, and you suddenly read: "… and we thought Him a leper." A leper? Where did he get that word "a leper"? That is strange! So you look back and see, "… we did esteem Him stricken." Well, you think, "There must be something very strange about this; I had better look it up in the concordance."

You begin to look through the concordance for the word *stricken* and you find Lamentations 4:9 says, "stricken through; to be stricken." Then in Isaiah 53:4 it says, "Yet we did esteem Him stricken, smitten of God, and afflicted." Do you know what that word is? It is "to touch, to come upon, to strike, or to plague." In Isaiah 53:8 it says, "For the transgression of my people was

He stricken." He was plagued! By this time you are very excited, and you begin to say, "I never knew!" Plagued, you see!

Now, can we find out if this word is used anywhere else in Scripture? In the concordance we find that it is the Hebrew word *nega*. In the back of the concordance every word used, both Hebrew and Greek, is listed alphabetically. When you look up the word *nega* you will find everything about it, as well as other places where it is used. For instance, it is the word used in Leviticus, chapters 13 and 14, not once but again and again and again in almost every single verse in those two chapters. It is the word *plague*.

Leviticus 13:2a says, "When a man shall have in the skin of his flesh a rising, or a scab, or a bright spot, and it become in the skin of his flesh the plague of leprosy ..." That is the word. In fact the Vulgate translators have gotten more of an idea of the meaning of this word "stricken" than perhaps we realise. When they translated it into Latin, Jerome thought about it for a long time: "Should we put stricken? If we put stricken, what will that mean to them? Will it mean anything to them?" He thought to himself, "The idea is plagued. Plagued with leprosy."

In other words, we thought that His being crucified like a criminal on the cross was because He was a sinner! But in fact it was "for the transgression that was due to my people" that He became a leper. He did become a leper, but He became a leper for us! So Jerome thought, "Now what shall I do? What Latin word shall I use? I know what I will put in. I will say, 'We did esteem Him a leper,' because, in fact, that is really what it means!"

So now you are investigating God's Word. Don't you think it will mean something more to you in the morning or evening when you are in your study reading your little bit of the Word? Don't you think a fresh revelation of the cross will break on you when you realise Jesus, the sinless one, became a leper for you? All my leprosy was placed on Him! Well, personally I think it is absolutely wonderful!

And then look at 1 Peter 5:7 again: "casting all thy care upon Him for He careth for you." Now as you consider that you might think, "Casting. Casting. Casting all your care upon Him." What does it mean, "casting all your care"? Well, look it up in the concordance, and this is what it says, "to hurl upon." Now, you can *cast* rubbish on the dustbin or upon the compost heap, but when you *hurl* something upon it, my word, you are getting rid of it, aren't you? You are really putting some energy into it! You are not just gently tipping it out, but you are getting hold of it and throwing it upon the rubbish heap.

Do you know what Peter said to the saints? He said, "Anxiety, care, worry is so clinging that the only way to get rid of it is to get hold of it and *hurl* it upon the Lord!" It is the only way to get rid of worry.

Some people think the scriptural way of dealing with worry is to be very genteel. So they worry and say to themselves, "be not anxious." Then it flits away for the moment and like a returning pigeon, back it comes into the mind. There it is again, and they are worrying again. They think, "No, no, no. I must not be anxious." Out it flits again, then gradually, like a pigeon, it comes back and it has come home to roost. Worry is a thing that comes home to roost. It comes back again and again to the dear old dovecot to sit there, back in its home. The only way to get rid of it is to take hold of the thing and hurl it upon the Lord! That means absolute determination! Take hold of the thing that is your anxiety and hurl it upon the Lord.

How are you going to find that out if you do not investigate God's Word? If you just read it as "casting" you might not realise the full force of it all. But when you have investigated the word, you discover what it means. So that is another thought. Do not only examine microscopically but also search out, investigate.

## Search

Of course, the last word is the one used in the Authorised Version—*search*. In other words, we are to search as one does for a lost brooch or a lost treasure. If you have a precious brooch or ring and one of the stones falls out, what do you do about it? You search everywhere for it! What happens when someone gets lost? There is an aerial search; planes go up to survey everything until they can find where the lost person is. You search for them.

This is what we are meant to do with God's Word. In Acts 17:11 we are told: "These were more noble than those in Thessalonica in that they searched the Scriptures daily." In other words, they really went through the Scriptures. It is not just a question of examining microscopically, investigating, tracing it right back to the source (as we have done on those two portions), but really searching through the Scriptures. It is really taking, as it were, an aerial survey of the whole thing, looking everywhere, really getting down to the job seriously and searching the thing out. That is serious business. So, the first thing is to search God's Word.

## Meditate

The second thing is to meditate upon God's Word. Joshua 1:8a, c: "This book of the law shall not depart out of thy mouth, but thou shalt meditate thereon day and night ... for then thou shalt make thy way prosperous, and then thou shalt have good success."

Psalm 1:2: "But his delight is in the law of the Lord; and on his law doth he meditate day and night." By the way, the word here is "'muse" or "mutter." The idea is of a man who is so lost in meditation that he is muttering to himself. He is sort of saying something like this, "Commit thy way unto the Lord—what does that mean? Commit thy way unto the Lord. Well, I suppose it means ..." He is so lost in meditation that he is chattering to himself. He is musing. He is talking as it were, turning it over in his heart and in his mind.

This word *meditate* is a lost art, and because it is a lost art, many a Christian's life is barren. Meditation is linked with refreshment, and somehow in my mind it is always linked with dew. When a person is quiet, dew falls. In Egypt and in the Middle East everything in the summer and for most of the winter is dependent on the dew. Sometimes that dew is so heavy early in the morning that it is almost a mist which passes through and leaves all the gum trees and everything else dripping for just a few minutes until the sun is out. But that moisture enables everything that is alive to live through another day. Have you ever seen the dew fall? The dew comes quietly, silently, when no one is about. The thing we associate with dew is *quietness*.

Then, what does this word *meditate* mean? There can be no hurry; that is all. People say to me, "That is impossible. I just cannot meditate; I live a very busy life." Of course, that is just the point.

Meditation does not mean that you have got to have two hours or even an hour. It just means that you are to take a grip upon yourself and say, "Ten minutes of this day is going to be spent in inactivity." That's all, just absolute silence. Even on a human scale some people do yoga and other things just simply because there is a lot of meditation involved in it. Whilst in many ways that may have not so much relation to the spiritual things, yet there is no doubt about it that there is a vital need in the human constitution for absolute quietness and silence.

What does it mean to meditate? It does not mean that you sit there with an empty mind. It means that you fill your mind with God's Word and sit quietly reflecting. You have got God's Word and you are thinking about it. You are not hurrying over it, but you are reflecting on it. That is the way revelation comes. It will not always come in a flash, but whilst you are reflecting, something will dawn on you.

I am sure there is something here that you and I have got to learn. It is no good grumbling about others, or about what you have been taught, or about the company that you are in here or elsewhere, or even the Lord Himself if you do not give time to meditate upon God's Word. I am putting it crudely, but you must give God's Word a chance to work, and meditation is the key. Time has got to be created for meditation because every single thing will come against it; but you have got to do it! You will find that the busiest lives are those that shut the door and sit down and think because they have got to! It is the only way through.

I would like to say one other thing about this quiet reflection and musing upon God's Word. How really rare it is to take some portion of God's Word and just sit and think about it. Now you see prayer, worship, and communion are linked with meditation. Have you ever thought in your time with the Lord of taking some portion of God's Word and just quietly turning it over in your mind and your heart with Him? I do not mean asking Him all the time, pleading with the Lord, or interceding. I just mean communing, talking about it. "Well Lord, 'Delight thyself in Thee,' what does that mean?" Think about it with the Lord.

"The secret of the Lord is with them that fear Him." Have you ever thought about it? Sit down and think of it. "Oh, dear Lord, You have got a secret. I wish that I could be in possession of Your secret. Do I really fear Thee, Lord?"

Meditation leads to worship. Sometimes we can worship the Lord from some portion of His Word we are meditating upon. We can bow down and worship the Lord and say, "Lord, how wonderful! How simply wonderful that is!"

That is meditation and it is a lost art! I hate to call it an art because somehow it seems as if it is a "thing." However, meditation should be part and parcel of the Christian life, a quite spontaneous and essential part of the Christian life. All I am saying is that in our studying and reading of God's Word there has got to be a place for prayer and worship and communion mingled in with it. It is God's Word and we need to remember that very much.

## Compare

And then there is this other word *compare*. How do we compare? First Corinthians 2:13: "... comparing spiritual things with spiritual" (Authorised Version). Second Peter 1:20: "No prophecy of scripture is of private interpretation," and in II Timothy 2:15: "... rightly handling or rightly dividing the word of God."

We have said that we need to compare scripture with scripture, remembering that the Bible is an unfolding revelation. We cannot just take one scripture and build a whole lot upon it. We must compare scripture with scripture.

How? Marginal references are one way. Another way is by the concordance. For instance, as you come up against something and look up the marginal references, you compare what other passages say about this particular matter.

I will give you an example from II Peter 1:21: "No prophecy ever came by the will of man: but men spake from God, being moved by the Holy Spirit." What does it mean, "being moved by the Holy Spirit"? Well, look up the marginal reference, I Peter 1:11: "Searching what time or what manner of time the Spirit of Christ which was in them did point unto, when it testified beforehand the sufferings of Christ ..." There is another scripture that throws light upon II Peter 1:21.

Then, look up II Samuel 23:2: "The Spirit of the Lord spake by me, (or in me). And his word was upon my tongue."

Luke 1:70: "As he spake by the mouth of his holy prophets that have been from of old."

Acts 1:16: "Brethren, it was needful that the scripture should be fulfilled, which the Holy Spirit spake before by the mouth of David ..."

When you follow through with these different references, you begin to discover that you have something else in the Word all being compared. Now you have got some idea of what it means to be moved by the Holy Spirit, you see. You are comparing it with other scriptures.

The concordance is another helpful way of comparing scripture with scripture. If you have a particular word and you want to make sure that it is the same original word that is translated, you look it up in the concordance. There you will find all the references to it, and if you follow them you can compare all of the different references.

Sometimes, it is a subject that you want to look up, and if you take a Bible dictionary, it will refer you to every part in God's Word where this particular subject is mentioned. In this way you compare matter with matter. You compare scripture with scripture, and you are preserved from unbalanced interpretation. All this is very, very important indeed.

Suppose you are reading in your study 1 Timothy 5:23, "Be no longer a drinker of water, but use a little wine for thy stomach's sake and thine often infirmities." You may well feel, especially if you like wine that here the Scripture tells us we must give up drinking water. Someone says, "God's Word is God's Word! Here God's Word says, "Be no longer a drinker of water." Well then, does that mean we must obey God's Word and give up water all together? We must become water abstainers? God's Word says to give up drinking water. "Be no longer a drinker of water." It goes on to positively tell us to use a little wine for thy stomach's sake.

Now I am using a rather absurd example, yet it goes to the root of the matter. This is the kind of thing that people do, taking truths to an extreme. They do not do it with this verse, but this is the kind of thing they do with a little phrase like this.

Exclusivism has taken a verse or two in II Timothy and built upon it a huge structure. Do you know what it is all built upon? "In a big house there are many vessels, some unto honor, some unto dishonor. If a man therefore purge himself from these, he shall be a vessel unto honor," (see II Timothy 2:20b–21a). Upon this one verse they have built this whole matter of separation from believers. It is to the point now that we heard the other day of known Christians, a sister and her own flesh-brother. When it came to teatime she said, "I will give you tea, but I shall have to have tea in this room, and you must have it in that room."

Someone says, "How can they do it?" Well you see, they have taken one or two verses such as the ones in II Timothy about "purging yourself from vessels of dishonour that you may be a vessel unto honour," forgetting what it says in Ephesians 4 about giving diligence to maintain the unity of the Spirit. Or forgetting what it says in I Corinthians 1 about I am of Paul, I am of Apollos, I am of Cephas, and I am of Christ—the exclusive position— overlooked entirely.

This is the danger and here we have got it in a rather, perhaps extreme way: "Be no longer a drinker of water, but use a little wine for thy stomach's sake." We must look up one or two other scriptures. Proverbs 20:1 says, "Wine is a mocker, strong drink a brawler; and whosoever erreth thereby is not wise." Now what do we say about that? "Wine is a mocker, strong drink a brawler and whosoever erreth thereby (it says in my margin 'reeleth thereby') is not wise." Again in chapter 21:17: "He that loveth pleasure shall be a poor man: he that loveth wine and oil shall not be rich."

You can see there is a lot more in Scripture about drink as well. You have got to take this scripture and that scripture and then bring them together. You have to understand that you cannot build a great doctrine on one scripture at the expense of the other. That is what we mean about comparing.

Let me give you another good example of this. Acts 13:48 is a good, classic example. "And as the Gentiles heard this, they were glad, and glorified the word of God: and as many as were ordained to eternal life believed." As you are reading your portion in the morning, you are very thrilled about it all, when suddenly you come to this and oh dear, dear, dear you are most upset. "As many as are ordained to eternal life believed."

Then you start to think: "Now what did brother so and so say at such and such a conference? I remember he said, 'Wherever you find this matter of fore-ordination, it is not connected with eternal life or salvation; it is connected with adoption as sons and being conformed to the image of Christ.'"

Then you look at this verse: "As many as were ordained to eternal life believed." You think: "Oh, I wonder if brother so-and-so has seen that verse?" Then you begin to wonder, "What is the point of praying in the prayer meeting for the unsaved?" Then in Romans 8:29 and 30 you see this: "For whom he foreknew, he also foreordained to be conformed to the image of his Son, that he might be the firstborn among many brethren: and whom he foreordained, them he also called: and whom he called, them he also justified: and whom he justified, them he also glorified."

"Oh!" you think, "I am afraid I have got to be a Calvinist. It is quite clear in God's Word that we are ordained unto eternal life." You can get very, very twisted on this matter. You can go to brother so-and-so and say, "I am very sorry, but I cannot work in the Sunday School anymore." "Oh!" the brother says, "you cannot work in the Sunday School anymore?" "No, no! I think it is entirely wrong. I believe that as many as are ordained unto eternal life will believe. We do not need to do anything; God will do it."

So you go off to someone else and say, "I am sorry, but I cannot go fishing (witnessing) anymore. I think fishing is all of the flesh. It is quite wrong. I believe that as many as are ordained unto eternal life will believe; they will be added to the church. All you have got to do is get things right at the centre and they will all pack in. You do not have to go out; you do not have to do anything."

Then after a little while you will start to worry about the brother who preaches the gospel on Sunday evening. You will say, "Really, I do not believe that is of the Spirit at all. How can he go out to the unsaved like that, preaching at them and saying to them, 'Come, come, come'? He should not say that! He should say, 'Look here! Those of you who are ordained unto eternal life will be saved.' The rest, we will just draw a curtain over them. Those of you who are ordained unto eternal life shall be saved." Do you see what I mean? In the end you will get to such a position that you cannot even pray.

Do you think that is absurd? It is not absurd. I can take you to a group in Richmond who have no Sunday School, no open-air meetings, no evangelistic outreach. Nothing at all. They have gone so far that they are not even sure that they themselves are saved. It is true. They are the strictest of the strict Baptists. Do you know that at the beginning of the 20th century they were a thriving company? How many of them are left? The whole work is gone and there are only about seven or eight of them left. The whole thing has been driven to an extreme, absolutely to an extreme! Of course, you can see that is why we need to compare scriptures.

Revelation 22:17b: "He that is athirst, let him come: he that will, let him take the water of life freely." Would you believe it? Now what am I going to do? "As many as he has ordained unto eternal life believed." "He that will, let him take of the water of life freely."

Matthew 11:28–29: "Come unto me, all ye that labour and are heavy laden, and I will give you rest. Take my yoke upon you, and learn of me; for I am meek and lowly in heart; and ye shall find rest unto your souls." It is amazing, isn't it? "Whosoever comes to me I will in no wise cast out" (see John 6:37).

We can take a scripture like Isaiah 53:12: "Yet he bare the sin of many." This is taken by people who believe this very much: "Ah," they say, "isn't that wonderful! That means He bare the sin of the elect—not the world."

However, elsewhere it says in 1 John 2:2 that He gave himself "for our sins; and not for ours only, but also for the whole world." This is what I mean by comparing scripture with scripture. You have to be careful. "He bare the sins of many" is a Hebrew phrase, as we would speak of "the many" meaning "the all." So you have got to compare and compare and bring both together. You have got to understand that somewhere the truth lies between the two all the time. You cannot build doctrine or great doctrinal structure on one scripture at the expense of another.

Spurgeon used to say, "In the pulpit I am an Arminian and in the prayer meeting I am a Calvinist. On my knees I say, 'Lord, save the elect,' and in the pulpit I say, 'Everyone who will, come.'" That is true. That is all we can do. This is a mystery. Somehow or other we have to be saved from going to extremes.

## Obey

We have said quite a lot about the vital importance of obedience to God's Word. Much, I think, hangs on small issues in this matter. When God speaks to us through His Word as we meditate, as we investigate and examine and search, as we compare scripture with scripture, as God speaks to us, we must be obedient. If we are not obedient we will have no further light. If anyone feels God's Word is dead to them, and they would say, "I have listened to what you have to say, but it does not touch me at all; God's Word does not mean a thing to me," I want to say to you just a simple thing: somewhere or other you have disobeyed. It is as simple as that. Somewhere or other you have disobeyed light. God refuses to speak another word until you are obedient to light given. When you are obedient to light given, you will see more light in the light. It will go on and go on and go on. The path of the just is a shining light that shines more and more to the perfect day (see Proverbs 4:18). That is how it ought to be, not growing darker and darker and more uncertain than ever, but going on into the light through all the storms and conflicts that are going on. However, you have got to be obedient to light. God is no trifler. You must not think that He can show you something at great cost and you turn your back on it and say "no," and then expect Him to show you anything more. He won't do it. Until you have got through that lesson, until you have learnt that lesson and are obedient to that lesson, no further light.

When Abraham built an altar and then fell, he went down into Egypt. God wonderfully brought him back from Egypt in the most amazing way, and he was taken back to the altar he left. There he had to offer again on the same altar. In other words,

God takes us back to the same point at which we rebelled or at which we fell. It is always the same. There is no further light until we learn the lesson.

I would like to say just one further thing about obedience: sometimes, an awful lot hangs on a small issue. Maybe it is something you just do not think is very important. Maybe it is about your dress. It might be a behaviour problem. It may be about your pleasure. It may be about your work. It may be about punctuality. It may be about the way that you contribute. To you it is so small. What does that matter with a great Almighty God in the heaven and me just a little creature here on earth? How can it have any effect? You do not know. Upon that little thing a world depends. I have found it again and again in my own experience, and I have seen it by observation. I can show you people who are right back in the far country and it all hung on a very small little issue to which they were not prepared to be obedient. They refused light and then things became dead. As it became dead they lived on past experience until they began to feel that they were hypocrites, they were play-acting, and they felt nothing meant anything to them anymore. Gradually, their hearts became stone inside, and in the end they began to rebel against the whole thing until suddenly they were gone.

Spurgeon once gave a wonderful illustration of this. He said he was out in Brighton one morning. A hundred years ago, of course, it was in the day of sailing ships, and there was a huge fleet out in the channel that was becalmed and couldn't move. All the folk in Brighton were coming out to stand on the cliffs along the front to watch the ships out there, some through telescopes, trying to identify them. Then the most amazing thing happened.

A sudden storm hit. In the night a terrific thunderstorm and squall hit, and when morning came the next day one third of the ships had vanished. They had gone down. Spurgeon could not believe that so many ships could go down, and he went to ask some old sailors about it. (These were wooden ships by the way.) They said, "It is quite simple. You see, barnacles grew on them and they never regularly cleaned off the barnacles." In the end, it was those things that had rotted the ships, and when the storm came, they could not stand up; they just went over and down."

Spurgeon preached an amazing sermon, "There Go the Ships." What a sermon! He spoke about all kinds of ships and he likened them to Christians. There were the tea ships, the gunpowder ships, this kind of ship and that kind of ship. He spoke of this illustration as an example of when the storm came and some of them went down.

That is how it does happen. I have often thought about it since. Suddenly a storm comes to a company or to individuals, and you look round and certain people who outwardly did not seem superficially to be failing, have gone. In the storm they have gone down. Actually, the rot had already set in many, many, many months before.

We need to be obedient, and God's Word is the key. "Ye are clean through the Word which I have spoken unto you" (John 15:3). God's Word keeps us clean. It keeps us in the light. It keeps us going on with Him It keeps us free. It keeps us growing. May God give us grace to approach this whole question of Bible reading and study seriously.

# Study Guides

## The Text of the Bible

We want now to consider the text of the Bible–the original languages of the text, its transmission over the centuries, and the ancient manuscripts containing that text. It has been the concern of scholars over the centuries to ascertain the exact text of Scripture, as it originally existed. We call these studies "Textual Criticism," and it is a science not confined to the Bible alone, but applied to many kinds of literature. Its aim is to determine the original text by studying all available manuscripts, material and evidence. Note the following:

### A. The Languages Used

At one time it was confidently thought that nothing was written before Moses, and many people questioned whether there was any writing even in his day. Now, however, we know that men have written for at least 5000 years, for we have actual specimens! It was a very strong Jewish tradition that men began to write in the generations immediately following Adam, and Enoch in particular is mentioned as one whom God used to record various matters (now contained in Genesis 1–4).

This matter of writing is important to us, for the Bible is God's Word written. We are told explicitly that Moses wrote at least part of the first five books (Exodus 17:14; 24:4; 34:27–28; Numbers 33:2; Deuteronomy 31:9, 22, 24), if not a good deal more! It is more than possible that Genesis in particular is based on a number of very ancient records written on clay tablets in language(s) other than Hebrew. If this is the case then Moses was not only a compiler and editor, but a translator as well! We have of course, a number of old sources used in compiling the Scriptures, which have now vanished. See Numbers 21:14; Joshua10:13; II Samuel 1:18; II Chronicles 9:29.

There are three languages used in the text of the Bible– Hebrew, Aramaic, and Greek. Nearly the whole Old Testament is in Hebrew, with some small passages in Aramaic whilst the whole New Testament is in Greek without exception.

| The Division of the Semitic Family of Languages | |
|---|---|
| North | Amorite & Aramaic |
| West | Canaanite, Moabite, Phoenician & Hebrew |
| East | Languages of Babylon & Assyria (Akkadian) |
| South | Languages of Arabia & Ethiopia |
| Note: The Most widely spoken Semitic language today is Arabic. | |

# i. Hebrew

It belongs to the Semitic family of languages and its Western group which included Canaanite, Moabite and Phoenician. It is not called Hebrew in the Old Testament but variously "the language of the lip of Canaan." Isaiah 19:18; "Jews language," Isaiah 36:11, Nehemiah 13:24. It is referred to as "Hebrew" in Rev. 9:11 and 16:16. In early days Hebrew had only dialect variations from Phoenician and Moabite. Although after the return from exile, Aramaic gradually became the vernacular of the people, Hebrew remained the sacred language (rather like Roman Catholic Latin!) and was used by the Rabbis in discussion and for writing. It has never died out, and in the last century has seen a remarkable revival becoming the official language of Israel.

# ii. Aramaic

It belongs to the northern group of Semitic language. It is called in the Old Testament "the Syriac language" e.g. Daniel 2:4 (it is often referred to in old books as Chaldee, mistakenly). It was the language of Syria and the upper regions of the Euphrates. It seems that by the eighth century BC, and certainly by Sennacherib's day (seventh century) Aramaic was the diplomatic language of the Assyrian Empire (see II Kings 18:26). It was to continue as the official language in the Persian Empire until its overthrow in 331 BC. In fact, a certain form of Aramaic was used in the Civil Service of the succeeding empires and has come to be called "Imperial Aramaic" (e.g. see Ezra). As we have said, it gradually superseded Hebrew as the spoken language of Palestine after the return from Babylon, and remained so until the seventh century AD! This does not mean that it was a younger language than Hebrew. It would seem clear that it was the original language of the Patriarchs before they finally settled in Canaan, and Hebrew became their tongue. One name in Genesis (31:47), one verse in Jeremiah (10:11) and some passages in Daniel (2:4–7:28) and Ezra (4:8–6:18; 7:12–26) are in Aramaic.

It was the language spoken everywhere in New Testament times in Palestine. It was both the language of the Lord, the Apostles and the early church in Palestine. We have some evidence of this in Aramaic words still in the New Testament cf Mark 5:41 (*Talitha Cumi*); 7:34 (*Ephphatha*); 15:34 (*Eloi, Eloi, lama sabachthani*); Acts 1:19 (*Akeldama*); I Corinthians 16:22 (*Marantha*). Also *Mammon, Abba, Golgotha, Gabbatha*. The Greek of the Gospels and some parts of Acts suggest their Aramaic background, and the possibility of older Aramaic records used in their writing e.g. Luke 1:5–2:52. Today Aramaic is still spoken by some Syrian, Iraqi and Persian Christians.

## iii. Greek

It was, however, neither Aramaic, nor Hebrew that was used for writing the New Testament, but Greek. From the time that Alexander the Great conquered the Persian Empire (331 BC), and the great Greek era began, Greek became increasingly the diplomatic language of the Empire, until in the New Testament times it was the "international language." Latin was used in the Roman Army, and even in Rome most people could speak Greek. Greek is not a Semitic language but belongs to the Indo-European family of languages. The Greek used in the New Testament is not classical Greek, but the Greek used in everyday life of the first century AD. It is often called Hellenistic Greek. It used to be fashionable to describe New Testament Greek as "Biblical or Jewish Greek!" Recently, most scholars have swung away from that position. In the light of new discoveries, the relation of New Testament Greek to the common Greek spoken and written everywhere at that time has become much clearer. Hellenistic Greek was a stage in the process of classical Greek to Modern Greek. Nevertheless, we must state emphatically that the Septuagint (LXX) version of the Old Testament had a tremendous influence upon New Testament Greek. The LXX used Greek words with Hebrew conceptions and construction. Indeed, it gave to some Greek terms a new outlook and meaning. It thus gave the New Testament Greek a particular flavour. We have also to add to this the influence of Aramaic.

## B. The Transmission of the Text

Note the word "Scripture", II Timothy 3:16, II Peter 1:20– not the spoken word, but the written! It thus implies the sovereign oversight of God in the writing down and transmission of His Word (esp. "Scripture might be fulfilled," John 13:18; 17:12 cf 10:35).

Until the invention of printing in the 15th century AD, the only mode of transmission was copying by hand. In fact, we would have no Bible, due to the perishable nature of the materials used, if it had not been for the continual painstaking copying over centuries. It is a singularly remarkable fact that our

Bible has been copied by hand, at least in part, for some 4400 years. We know that in the Ancient World from at least 2000 BC men received training to become expert copyists. It was a very important function in national, as well as religious life.

iii. We must also remember the tremendous regard and reverence with which from the beginning the sacred text was handled by scribes and copyists. This has no doubt influenced the comparative standard of accuracy. See Josephus, *Against Apion I*, p. 609. We have to admit that there have been some copyists' mistakes in words, and in numbers, partly explained by the nature of Hebrew Script (e.g. no punctuation, no vowels, and letters standing for numbers).

As can be seen, the result of such errors is to produce alternative or variant reading, not to be confused with actual shades of meaning in a word itself. For example Psalm 100:3 Authorised Version (KJV), cf. American Standard Version; Isaiah 9:3; Rev 1:5, "washed" or "loosed" depends on one letter. In fact, considering the period of time covered, the complexity of some of the records, the amount of the material, it is a real wonder that the mistakes are so few and unimportant. Not one single doctrine is affected in the whole Bible; the major themes and indeed the minor are unimpaired. See F.F. Bruce *The Books and The Parchments* (p. 180). When one remembers that even since printing, mistakes do often get through to publication (e.g. Psalm 119:161, old edition of Bible – "Printers" for "princes"; Exodus 20:14 – omission of

# Difficulties in the Hebrew Script

i. Lack of Punctuation in Hebrew text

See Isaiah 40:3 as it would look originally:
> *The voice of him that crieth in the wilderness*
> *prepare ye the way of the Lord make straight*
> *in the desert a highway for our God*

Here is the text in the Authorised King James Version:
> *The voice of him that crieth in the wilderness,*
> *Prepare ye the way of the Lord, make straight*
> *in the desert a highway for our God.*

Here again is the same text in the American Standard Version:
> *The voice of one that crieth, Prepare ye in the*
> *wilderness the way of Jehovah; make level*
> *in the desert a highway for our God*

Refer to page 25 for more, but you can see the difficulty in the decision of where to punctuate a verse like the above.

See as well John 9:3. The American Standard Version, Authorised Version KJV, and Revised Version all have the following punctuation:

*Jesus answered, Neither did this man sin, nor his parents: but that the works of God should be made manifest in him.* ASV

Find the Peshitta Version for a comparison:

*Jesus said to them, neither did he sin nor his parents. But that the works of God might be seen in him, I must do the works of him who sent me while it is day.* Peshitta (Syriac Version)

See page 59–60 for more discussion

See also Romans 9:5. The punctuation of the Authorised Version KJV, American Standard Version, match the Revised Version:

*whose are the fathers, and of whom is Christ as concerning the flesh, who is over all, God blessed for ever. Amen.* RV

Compare the Revised Standard Version:

*to them belong the patriarchs, and of their race, according to the flesh, is the Christ. God who is over all be blessed for ever. Amen.*

When you have the full stop before "God who is over all be blessed for ever" the meaning of the verse is different.

ii. No vowels in Hebrew (see p. 24-26)

## An example for explanation

For example the English word *water* would be written as:

WTR

Imagine an error occurred with just one letter and it became:

WFR

*Water* then would likely be translated as *wafer*!!

## Pronunciation example

Hebrew: YHWH

English: Jehovah

We really do not actually know the pronunciation of this since the vowels were never written!

## An example of an error that occurred

*By faith Jacob, when he was dying, blessed each of the sons of Joseph; and worshipped, leaning upon the top of his staff. Hebrews 11:21 ASV*

*And he said, Swear unto me: and he sware unto him. And Israel bowed himself upon the bed's head. Genesis 47:31 ASV*

Here you find the Hebrew for bed and staff are both MTH (Mittah/Matteh) so there was a mistake in the translation.

"not" – hence "wicked Bible"), it is no mean feat that the Bible is so free of mistakes.

# C. The Ancient Manuscripts

## The Ancient Manuscripts of Old Testament Text

i. The problem of establishing the correct Hebrew text of the Old Testament is not an easy one, for only comparatively late manuscripts survive. We have no full manuscripts, earlier than ninth century AD, although we have some books and fragments much earlier (Dead Sea Scroll etc.) All the extant Hebrew manuscripts of the Old Testament contain the Masoretic Text. The Masoretes ("transmitters" from Masorah – 'Tradition') were Jewish Rabbis and scholars who edited the Hebrew Old Testament from the sixth to the ninth century AD. There is a manuscript of the Pentateuch in the British Museum usually dated ninth century AD, and one of the prophets in Leningrad dated 916 AD. There is also one of the whole Old Testament from early 11th century AD, another as old at Oxford, and another older at Aleppo! All these belong to the same family tracing their lineage to the same basic text. That there were other such texts is evidenced from the variations in ancient versions such as the LXX, Syriac, etc.

ii. The Masoretes were responsible for introducing vowel signs and punctuation into the text. They fixed the Hebrew text to exactness and observed the strictest rules for copying. Their work was truly painstaking! For example, when a book was copied the Hebrew letters were counted and the middle letter given, for both the copy and the original.

If they did not tally, the copy was rejected. Similarly with the words!! Their guiding principle was to hand on the text as they received it. It was because of their tremendous reverence for it, and the high standard of accuracy, that we have so few really early manuscripts!! The Rabbis disposed of the old worn copies by burying them in consecrated ground. Often before they were so interned, they were stored in a room in the Synagogue called "Genizah" (hiding place). It has been due to some old manuscripts being overlooked in these rooms, that we now have some of them at all, such as the Cairo Genizah.

The Masoretic Text itself was based on the work of the Talmudists of second century and onwards. (The Talmud is a Jewish commentary upon the Old Testament containing the most ancient traditions, stories, observations and explanations.)

Thus we can trace the Hebrew Text to within a century of our Lord. Indeed, in all probability we can say that we have the same text as He used. But have we any other means of checking this text? Yes, we have!

*a. The Samaritan Pentateuch*

The Samaritan Pentateuch is a version in Hebrew of Genesis to Deuteronomy. It is unquestionably derived from a very ancient text different to the Masoretic, which must date from at least the fifth century BC. The earliest manuscripts extant date from the 10th and 13th Centuries AD. It deviates from the Masoretic Text but in substance testifies to its essential accuracy. Because of its antiquity it is an invaluable check on the Pentateuch.

### b. The Dead Sea Scrolls

The discovery in 1947 at Qumran of a large number of Biblical manuscripts has greatly influenced the whole study of the Text. These manuscripts are earlier than the Masoretic Text by 900–1000 years! They include a copy of Isaiah (full); a copy of Habakkuk (full); another of Isaiah (a third only) and fragments of every other Old Testament book except Esther, some books being represented several times. They constitute another independent witness to the substantial reliability we have.

### c. The Septuagint (LXX)

This is the oldest version of the whole Old Testament being a translation into Greek, made at Alexandria, in the third century BC. It was for the benefit of the Greek-speaking Jews. It was supposed to have been made by 72 Elders in 72 days – hence LXX. It is generally considered to be fearful Greek! One scholar has called it "Hebrew in disguise." Its great value lies in its being an independent check on the Masoretic Text, for it embodies a basic text other than Masoretic. It varies in different places (especially Samuel and Kings), but essentially it substantiates the Masoretic Text. Sometimes LXX corrects it; generally the Masoretic Text proves superior. The best and earliest manuscripts of LXX date from the 4th and 5th Centuries AD, some four centuries earlier than the Masoretic manuscripts.

### d. The Syriac, or Peshitta (Simple)

This was a version of the Old Testament in Syriac from Hebrew made probably in the second or third century AD. It has been revised in light of LXX, so it is not so valuable a check. Nevertheless, it is another witness added to the others for the reliability of our Text. The earliest full manuscripts of the Syriac date from sixth–seventh century AD.

### e. The Latin Vulgate (Popular)

This was a translation of the whole Bible into Latin by Jerome, the greatest scholar amongst Church Fathers, made about 400 AD. The Old Testament was a translation direct from Hebrew some 500 years before our extant Masoretic manuscripts. With the other versions it proves an added check upon Masoretic Text. What is generally agreed by all scholars is that the Masoretic Text, upon which our Old Testament is based, is superior to the others, being more reliable, trustworthy and accurate. See F.F. Bruce *Second Thoughts on Dead Sea Scrolls* (p. 69).

Sometimes these versions (LXX, Vulgate, Peshitta) help us in determining the meaning of a verse which has become corrupted or seems obscure.

### a. Zechariah 13:6

"wounds in Thy hands" in the Authorised Version (KJV); "between thine arms" in the Revised Version and New American Standard Bible; "on your back" in the Revised Standard Version and compare to "in your hands" in the Syriac, "between thy hands"

---

6 Ask they, What wounds be these in thy clasped hands?✳ Thus wounded was I, he shall answer, in the house of my friends.✳

Literally, 'between thy hands', a difficult phrase most inadequately interpreted by some moderns as meaning 'on thy back'. If the sacred author had meant 'between thy arms', he would surely have said so, as in IV Kg. 9.24.

LXX, "what wounds be these in thine clasped hands" Vulg. Knox. See Knox's footnote:

## b. Isaiah 53:10

"Thou ... make His soul an offering for sin" Authorised Version (KJV), American Standard Version, Revised Version (mg. alternative given) "When He makes Himself an offering ..." Revised Standard Version "He laid down His life an offering for sin" Syriac. "His life laid down for guilt's atoning" Vulg. Knox. "If He would render Himself as a guilt offering" NASB.

## c. Genesis 4:8

"Cain talked with Abel" Authorised Version (KJV). "Cain told his brother" Revised Version, American Standard Version, New American Standard Bible, LXX, Syriac – "Cain said to Abel, 'Let us go out into the field or plain." Vulgate – "Cain said ... 'Let us go out together." Obvious ommission in Hebrew Masoretic Text from next sentence "and it came to pass when they were in the field."

Moses built an altar and called the name of it, The LORD is my banner, [16] saying, "A hand upon the banner of the LORD! The LORD will have war with Am'alek from generation to generation."

**18** Jethro, the priest of Mid'ian, Moses' father-in-law, heard of all that God had done for Moses and for Israel his people, how the LORD had brought Israel out of Egypt. [2] Now Jethro, Moses' father-in-law, had taken Zippo'rah, Moses' wife, after he had sent her away, [3] and her two sons, of whom the name of the one was Gershom (for he said, "I have

*That is* Proof  *That is* Contention  *Cn:* Heb obscure
**17. 14:** Deut. 25. 17–19; 1 Sam. 15. 2–9.  **18. 3, 4:** Acts 7. 29.

An example of a correction in RSV is Exodus 17:16. See in text on the word "banner". In some versions you find kêç (throne) , while others such as the Samaritan version say nêç (a banner)

נֵ ס nêç          כֵּ ס kêç

An example of similar lettering leading to a question of which word was intended, which led the RSV to make a correction.

## d. Exodus 17:6

The Hebrew here seems obscure. "The Lord hath sworn ..." Authorised Version (KJV), Revised Version, American Standard Version, and New American Standard Bible. See margin. Hebrew literally, "A hand upon the throne of the Lord." Revised Standard Version – "A hand upon the banner of the Lord" (a correction, see footnote.) LXX "With a secret hand the Lord wages war upon Amalek." Vulgate. Knox "He cried, 'lift up your hands to the Lord's throne.' The Lord declares war against Amalek." (see footnote "The Hand of the Throne of the Lord, and the war of the Lord, will be against Amalek.") See Revised Standard Version note z to left:

Sometimes these versions can throw more light upon the meaning of a verse: cf Isaiah 53:4 "stricken" – Vulg. Knox "A leper." Hebrew translated "stricken" can mean plagued, and we find it in Lev 13:14 (see e.g. v2).

## Ancient Manuscripts of New Testament Texts

1. The problem of establishing the correct New Testament Text is comparatively easier than the Old Testament, since we have a large number of Greek manuscripts preserving many variant forms of the original text. We have copies of the Greek New Testament written in the fourth century AD, quite substantial parts from the third century and some fragments from the second. The oldest fragment (of one of the Gospels) dates from 100–150 AD. In all there are manuscripts of the whole or part of the New Testament numbering more than 4000. Thus it can be seen that there is a large amount of material through which we can determine the original New Testament text. Nevertheless, there is one sense at least in which determining the New Testament text is more difficult than the Old Testament. Some so-called Christian scribes seem to have had no scruples about adding, omitting, or changing what seemed to them best!! This the Jewish Rabbis would not have dreamt of doing! Thus, sometimes because of heresies or for some other reason, verses were made "clearer" or more emphatic, or omitted or added!! It is a good thing that we have so many manuscripts extant by which we can judge what was the original e.g. 1 John 5:7–8 Authorised Version (KJV). Note the Revised Version, American Standard Version, Revised Standard Version, New English Bible and Syriac omit entirely both in text and footnotes. It appears in no early or good Greek manuscripts. Its earliest appearance (as far as at present we can judge) dates from the Latin writer, Priscillian, 385 AD, and thereafter in old Latin manuscripts. Mr. Knox says in footnote "The Latin manuscripts may have preserved true text."

In the light of this, it needs to be emphasized that we have **ii** more evidence for the original text of New Testament than any other work which has come down to us from the Ancient World. (See Westcott *"The Lessons From Revised Version"* p. 205, 210 and Revised Standard Version preface, page six.)

The most important manuscripts we have, come from **iii** the 4th–6th Centuries AD. Amongst these are:

## a. Codex Sinaiticus
Fourth century AD manuscripts of the whole Bible, now in the British museum. Parts of the Old Testament are missing.

## b. Codex Vaticanus
This has approximately the same date as the above. It is missing Hebrews from verse 9:14 to the end, the Pastoral letters, Philemon, and Revelation. It is in the Vatican library.

## c. Codex Alexandrinus
Fifth century AD manuscripts also in a British Museum.

Scholars today tend to divide all this material into five **iv** basic families representing the original text, while remembering that they are not independent of one another.

## a. The Byzantine (Syrian)
Known often as the "Received Text". It underlies the Authorised Version (KJV) based on *Codex Alexandrinus*. From fourth century AD.

### b. The Alexandrian (Neutral)

Thought often to be nearest to original text. Based on *Codex Sinaiticus* and *Vaticanus*. It underlies Revised Version and American Standard Version. From second century AD.

### c. The Western

This is the text of the old Latin manuscript. More recently scholars have felt this is nearer to the original than first thought. Not later than 150 AD.

### d. The Ceaserean

It is not easy to determine this. Some think it is a correction of the Western by Alexandrian.

### e. The Antiochian

The old Syriac Version was based on this. It also cannot be later than 150 AD.

V. Are there any other ways of checking the orginal text? Yes, we have:

### a. Early version of the New Testament

The most important of these are Latin, Syriac and Coptic dating from the second and the third century AD.

### b. Quotations of the New Testament by early writers

Principally Greek, Latin and Syriac writers from the 2nd–4th Centuries AD.

Our latest versions e.g. Revised Standard Version and New English Bible, etc are now based on all these, each variant reading being considered on its merits and no one particular family is being favoured. The English Authorised Version (KJV) of 1611 was based on the "Received Text", which was derived by Erasmus from a few late manuscripts and published at Basel in 1516. The most important manuscripts (*Sinaiticus* and *Vaticanus* and others) had not been discovered. This edition of the Greek text was substantially the Byzantine based on the *Codex Alexandrinus*. It included a comparatively small number of verses or phrases and one passage, not represented in the earliest and most reliable manuscripts. On the other hand, the Revised Version, American Standard Version, Revised Standard Version and the New English Bible omits these altogether, or relegate them to footnotes if there is some possibility of their representing the original text. For example:

*a. 1 John 5:7–8*
omitted all together by all

*b. John 7:53–8:11*
The Revised Version and American Standard Version keep it in text but have footnote: "Most of old manuscripts omit this passage: those which contain it vary from each other." Revised Standard Version places whole passage in footnotes. New English Bible places it on its own at end of John's Gospel, with footnote: "... has no fixed place in ancient witnesses." Some do not contain it at all, some place it after Luke 21:38; John 7:36, 52; or John 21:24.

### c. John 5:3–4

The Revised Version, American Standard Version, Revised Standard Version, and New English Bible, all place it in footnotes.

### d. Acts 8:37

The Revised Version, American Standard Version, Revised Standard Version, New English Bible and the New American Standard Bible also place this verse in footnotes.

**vii.** Sometimes the various versions will help us to understand what is meant. For example:

### a. Revelation 21:6

Authorised Version (KJV): "It is done."
The Revised Version, American Standard Version, and New English Bible: "They are come to pass." or "already fulfilled." The Revised Standard Version and New American Standard Bible go back to the Authorised Version (KJV) rendering. To me the Latin Vulgate (Knox) is the best; "it is over!"

### b. John 9:3, 4

A question of punctuation! The Authorised Version (KJV), Revised Version, American Standard Version, Revised Standard Version, and the New English Bible, follow the same punctuation. "But that works of God …" linked to preceding sentence. The Syriac Version links it to the following sentence. Does that embody the true meaning?

*c. Romans 9:5*

The Authorised Version (KJV), Revised Version, and American Standard Version give one form; the Revised Standard Version and New English Bible another. The Vulgate and Syriac favour former quite emphatically.

# D. Conclusion

When one remembers the 4400 years of copying by hand, the complexity of many of the records, the amount of material involved, the generally unscientific way (to us now!) in which these things were approached and handled, the human factors of failure, weakness, and inefficiency, the ravages of time and war, the perishable nature of the materials used, the desire of heresies to conform the text to their own convictions, and sometimes the equally great desire of orthodoxy to rule out any embarrassing Scriptures, it is a miracle that we have so few real points of variation in the text.

In fact it is singularly remarkable, considering all the evidence we have, that we hold in our hands today a text of both the Old Testament and the New Testament, which is substantially and essentially that which was originally written, and to whose accuracy all the latest discoveries testify! Furthermore, when we bring all points of doubt we have in the text, due to any mistake copying or human failing, and place them together, we discover that no major or minor theme of the Bible is impaired in any way, nor one single doctrine affected.

All this cannot be explained other than by the sovereign oversight of God in a most amazing way. We have in this volume a miracle indeed as great, if not greater than the construction of the heavens, or the very design of life; certainly more wonderful than any sensational healing or raising from the dead. The presence of this Book today is an indication of the presence of God in history and human affairs. Indeed we have enough to try our faith, and enough to bring us to our knees in a marvelling trust!

## Questions

1. What do we mean by "Textual Criticism," and why is writing so important to those who want to learn about God?

2. Which of the ancient versions of the Old Testament is the most important? State why it is the most important, and explain how these ancient versions help us in our understanding of the Old Testament.

3. If someone doubted the reliability of the Old and New Testaments, saying that because they were handed down from one generation to another they must have altered considerably, how would you answer him?

4. In your own words, compare the importance of the Hebrew and Aramaic languages.

5. Why is it so much easier to establish correct New Testament text?

6. a. What effect, if any, have the different versions of Old and New Testaments had upon the doctrines, and the major minor themes of the Bible?

b. What do you know about 1 John 5:7–8, John 7:53–8:11, and John 5:3–4, from the footnotes in modern versions of the Bible? Is the meaning of these verses in any way affected?

7. Why is the use of the word "Scripture" in certain verses of the Bible so remarkable?

8. What are the most important manuscripts which we have, of the New Testament Text?

9. What was "The Received Text"?

# How to Study the Bible

We have now looked at many aspects of the Bible – authority, revelation, inspiration; its aim and scope; its structure and growth; the text and its transmission; the history of the English versions etc. It remains for us to consider the way we should approach the personal reading and study of God's Word.

*i. The need to be careful not to substitute books on or about the Bible for the Bible itself!*

This is a danger anyone can fall easily into – reading and studying books on or about the Bible, and not the Bible itself! Such books of course, have their place, but if substituted for the Bible, they become positively dangerous.

The thing to remember and do is to READ and study God's Word itself above all else. It is a strange thing that we often have an aversion to reading the Bible–yet we can spend hours on newspapers, novels etc, or Christian books but not the Bible itself! Nevertheless Bible study can become not only vital and valuable, but enthralling, if approached in the right way.

Thus the first things to remember are:

i. We must read God's Word itself.

ii. Determination is needed to ignore feelings and make time for it.

*ii. The need to take Bible reading and study seriously.*

We must:

- Search or investigate

Acts 17:11. God's Word needs to be searched out and thoroughly investigated. It is like a mine of precious things.

- Meditate

    Joshua 1:8; Psalm 1:2. We need to give time for reflection and much thought upon God's Word. It is food to be digested.

- Compare

    1 Corinthians 2:13; II Peter 1:20; II Timothy 2:15. We need to compare Scripture with Scripture, remembering it is an unfolding revelation.

- Obey

    James 1:22; John 7:17; God's Word is to be obeyed! There will never be any further light until light given is obeyed. God's Word is not to be trifled with!

### iii. The need continually, in Bible reading and study, of prayerful reliance upon the Holy Spirit.

The Bible is mere literature to the natural mind—a great mass of religious law, story and doctrine. Its real meaning is hidden to the natural man. Indeed, it is a closed book. 1 Corinthians 2:12–14 cf also II Corinthians 3:14–16. Hence our need of the Holy Spirit John 16:13, 14 cf. 14:26 Ephesians 1:16–18 and 1 John 2:27. Never study the Word of God without first praying for the Holy Spirit's gracious ministry of guidance and enlightenment.

### iv. The need of humility in our approach to the Bible.

When we come against some thing we don't understand in God's Word, and it does not become clear after asking the Lord for understanding, leave it for the time being. Concentrate on what the Lord is showing you. In His time, you will be given understanding on the difficulty.

### v. The helpfulness of Bible aids.

- The concordance or word dictionary: It is better to invest in the more comprehensive type e.g. Young's. We need to remember that all are built on Authorised Version (KJV) wording. Note also Vine's Dictionary of Words, and Bullinger.
- Bible Dictionary: This is invaluable if you would understand Biblical matters e.g. customs etc.
- English Dictionary: This will often help us in our understanding.
- Marginal references. These are best in Revised Version and American Standard Version. They are invaluable e.g. Exodus 13:21 mg. refs. Also see footnotes in the Revised Version, American Standard Version, and Revised Standard Version for alternative meanings or variant readings.

### vi. Devotional reading of the Bible

We can never over-emphasize the need to regard God's Word as our spiritual food. We thus need to take some part of it each day and thoroughly digest it.

It is good to have a definite scheme or plan of reading rather than be haphazard. E.g. There are many schemes you can choose from or take one book and read some verses per day.

Give time for reflection over your daily passage; look up the marginal references; find out the meaning of the words, which are important. Here the American Standard Version and even J.N. Darby's version are important versions. The Amplified can be very helpful here too! Indeed if it is a short passage, comparing the various versions can be most helpful and instructive.

This is an essential form of Bible study and reading if we would ever grasp the overall theme or meaning of particular books. In this kind of study, we need to take a book and read it right through from beginning to end without a break, ignoring chapter and verse altogether. Some of the smaller books and letters take very little time to read through, e.g. Ephesians, 1 Peter etc. Even a large book like Job only takes two hours.

It is however, hard to read the Bible like this in the Authorised Version (KJV) or even the Revised Version. For the New Testament Phillips is very helpful. For the Old Testament, see the Revised Standard Version and the Living Bible. Read through a book in these different versions and gradually you will grasp the overall theme. In this type of study, some understanding of authorship, date and background is often helpful.

### vii. Analytical Study of the Bible

This is an absolutely exhaustive way of studying God's Word, and one of the most valuable. It is not so much concerned with the book and its overall theme, rather the meaning of each phrase. Thus it is a verse by verse, phrase by phrase method of study, using cross references, concordances, and other versions.

### viii. Other Ways of Studying the Bible

- Topical

For example: Types or symbols (dove, vine); places (Hebron, Jordan); events (Exodus, etc); occurrences of a certain word (worship, glory, etc).

- Biographical

  for example: Demas, Philemon 24; Colossians 4:14; II Timothy 4:10; David compared with his Psalms.

- Prophecy

  for example: Messianic and otherwise; fulfilled and unfulfilled.

## Questions

1. What, would you say is the greatest danger which faces us as we come to study the Bible?

2. What are the main difficulties which we must overcome if we are to study God's Word meaningfully?

3. What Bible aids do you find to be most helpful?

4. What is our spiritual food, and what must we do each day to be properly fed spiritually?

5. What is the difference between Comprehensive Study of the Bible, and Analytical Study of the Bible?

6. Have you ever tried Meditation of the Bible? If so, has it helped you, and how?

7. In which ways can God's Word meet us?

8. Which are the four things we must do if we are to undertake serious Bible reading and study?

9. Do you take notes or write out passages of the Bible in your own reading and study of God's Word? If the answer is yes, in what way has this helped you?

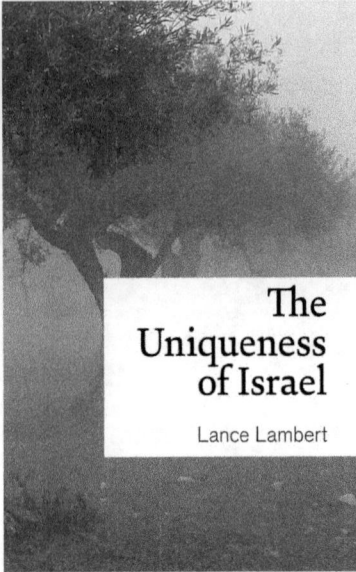

## The Uniqueness of Israel

Woven into the fabric of Jewish existence there is an undeniable uniqueness. There is bitter controversy over the subject of Israel, but time itself will establish the truth about this nation's place in God's plan. For Lance Lambert, the Lord Jesus is the key that unlocks Jewish history He is the key not only to their fall, but also to their restoration. For in spite of the fact that they rejected Him, He has not rejected them.

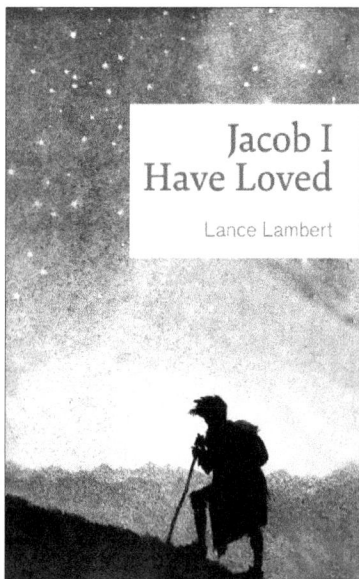

## Jacob I Have Loved

When God deals with us it is often in deeply mystifying ways. There is no greater example of how God shapes a person than through the remarkable story of Jacob. *Jacob I Have Loved* is an outstanding illustration of God's desire to utterly transform our fallen inner nature. Despite a twisted, deceiving, and sinful heart, Jacob nonetheless inherited God's richest blessings and became one of the patriarchs of our faith. Herein lies one of the Bible's great mysteries. His story is an integral part of the history of divine redemption. This book is about the power of God to transform a human life.

Jacob's story is our story.

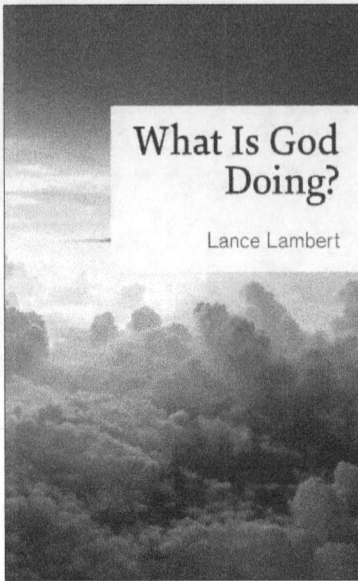

What Is God
Doing?

Lance Lambert

## What is God Doing?

Throughout the ages, God has been doing one thing which is all to do with His great purpose. As we survey the move of God throughout church history with its apparent ebb and flow, it becomes clear that not even the powers of hell can deter God from preparing the bride and building the eternal city.

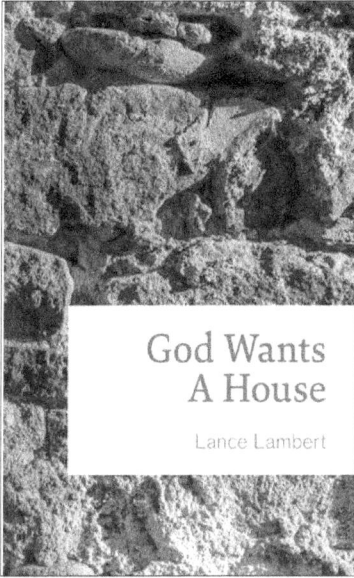

## God Wants a House

Where is God at home? Is He at home in Richmond, VA? Is He at home in Washington? Is He at home in Richmond, Surrey? Is He at home in these other places? Where is God at home? There are thousands of living stones, many, many dear believers with real experience of the Lord, but where has the ark come home? Where are the staves being lengthened that God has finally come home? In God Wants a House Lance looks into this desire of the Lord, this desire He has to dwell with His people. What would this dwelling look like? Let's seek the Lord, that we can say with David, "One thing have I asked of Jehovah, that will I seek after: that I may dwell in the house of Jehovah all the days of my life, To behold the beauty of Jehovah, And to inquire in his temple."